The
Drake Diner
Murders

By Pete Hale
with Jim Rowley

,

Special credit goes to retired Des Moines Police Department Detective James Rowley, who encouraged me to undertake this project, and without whose knowledge and firsthand experience in the case, could not have been accomplished. I would like to give special thanks to current Des Moines Police Chief Judy Bradshaw and *The Des Moines Register* for their cooperation. Thanks as well to my brother David Hale, who is a writer and photographer, for his support and thoughtful collaboration with us both in writing the story and editing the visual graphics.

Pete Hale with Jim Rowley

On November 29, 1992, two people were shot to death in cold blood at the Drake Diner in Des Moines Iowa. This is a true story of that notorious crime and the police investigation that followed. Police files, public records and interviews with those involved were used in the writing of this book. A few names of people incidental to the story have been changed to protect their privacy.

"Every now and then one event shapes a whole community, or even a state or a nation. Last Sunday's shootings at the Drake Diner had that effect on Des Moines. Waves of revulsion over the coldbloodedness (sic) of the crime sent different people's thoughts down different paths. Some dwelt on the gun, a hugely powerful weapon. Meanwhile across the city, black men girded themselves for all the suspicious eyes and fearful faces. Those who live nearby felt new fear with no suspect apprehended for so long."

Staff Editorial – *The Des Moines Register*
Saturday, December 5th, 1992

Prologue

OCTOBER 9, 1992

THE LAST CLASS on Friday afternoon was over. That was a big relief for both of the girls. They stopped outside school and talked with friends about what everybody was doing for the weekend. But the girls didn't divulge much about their plans to meet up with two boys. They had the whole weekend to fool around. The two guys that they were linking up with were a new challenge, but the girls definitely liked them. They got into the car and sped out of the school parking lot headed for home.

"We need to be careful. Can you tell if they're gone yet?"

"Oh, I can tell."

The parents were leaving their country home for the weekend. Her parents repeatedly told her that nobody was to be in the house while they were gone.

"Did your old man give you a lecture?"

"Yes. So what! We just have to be careful. What they don't know won't hurt them. I want to have a good time. I've been looking forward to this all week."

As the girls approached the house on the road, they slowed the car to a near stop so they could survey the scene. The weekenders had left so the girls parked the car in the middle of the driveway as the signal that it was clear for the boys.

They unlocked the door and went in. The dogs greeted them at the door. The house was rustic but comfortable.

Handmade curtains, wildlife art prints framed on the walls, a wall of books and antiques, a wood-burning stove – primarily masculine decor.

"Oh, the heat feels good. Did they stock the fridge for you again?"

"Ya', they always make sure there's plenty in there. The guys are bringing the party goods."

"Are you on the pill?"

"Oh, God, yes! If anything happened, my dad would friggin' kill me!"

They waited for the boys and talked. Occasionally one or the other would rise and anxiously go to the window. An hour passed. It was getting dark. The sun was going down earlier this time of year. The dogs were watered and fed. They went into the kitchen and took a frozen pizza out of the freezer. Suddenly there was the sound of car tires on the gravel road. Going to the window, the girls saw approaching headlights.

"I hope this isn't your mom and dad coming back."

"They're not coming back! You always freak out!"

It was the boys. They parked in the driveway and the girls could hear them laughing loudly as they walked toward the house. The girls opened the door and invited them in. Each of the boys had a full grocery sack.

"What you got there?"

The taller of the two boys said, "We got four twelve-packs of beer, a bottle of Chivas we 'appropriated', two ounces of excellent weed and a little coke! That damn dog gonna growl at us again?"

"No, I put the dogs in the other room."

The boys took their coats off. The girl whose parents were out of town was excited to see this particular boy again. She thought he was different from the other boys she knew. He was hip. He was mysterious and full of surprises. But she had surprises, too. They were prepared to enjoy each other for the weekend. The party was on.

FRIDAY, OCTOBER 1, 1976

DES MOINES POLICE DISPATCHERS received a call for help from two young women calling from a phone booth at 17th and Crocker Street. The women were frantic and begging for police help. Two men in a car nearby were frightening them. Police dispatchers radioed a close-by black-and-white to respond. The responding officers were Des Moines Policemen Michael Nehring and James Osterquist.

The marked police car arrived at the scene quickly. The girls pointed to a late model Lincoln that was parked and running near the phone booth. The officers approached the Lincoln from both sides. Suddenly, the passenger drew a large caliber handgun and opened fire on both officers. Nehring was hit first, then Osterquist. Officer Nehring fell to the ground on the driver's side from the first volley, very badly wounded. Officer Osterquist, hit three times, lost his balance and fell to the curb on the passenger side. The shooter climbed over the driver of the Lincoln, jumped out of the car and ran south. Osterquist managed to get back on his feet momentarily, draw his service revolver and fire several shots at the fleeing suspect before he fell to the ground and lost consciousness.

The Drake Diner, Des Moines, IA

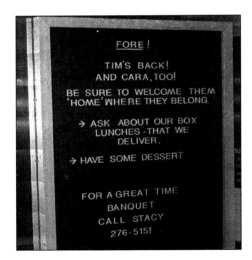

Welcome Home sign in the entrance to the diner
November 29, 1992

Chapter One

LATE NOVEMBER had finally brought cold weather to Iowa. On the Sunday following Thanksgiving it drizzled all day. There was a real chill in the air when darkness set in. Jeff Hughes and his wife, Julie, were driving home on University Avenue.

"So where do you want to stop to eat?"

Julie answered, "I'd like to hit the Drake Diner if it's not too crowded. No more leftover turkey!" The Drake Diner was one of the hippest, most popular spots in Des Moines.

"It'll be packed," Jeff said.

"Go down Twenty-Fifth Street and we'll check."

Jeff had the windshield wipers on intermittently. He turned off of University and went south toward the diner. Julie looked toward the building through the haze. The moment it was visible through the drizzle she said, "Not bad."

He turned the car around in the driveway and parked on the street. They walked in and noticed a banner that read "FORE! TIM'S BACK! AND CARA TOO! BE SURE TO WELCOME THEM HOME WHERE THEY BELONG!" Jeff looked to the right at the full booths and counter. The aroma of onions and garlic filled the air. The place buzzed with conversation, fun and laughter. It didn't seem to Jeff like there were enough cars in the parking lot for the number of people inside. People were standing in the entryway waiting to be seated. There was a ten-minute wait. Members of the Drake University basketball team, The Drake Bulldogs, were coming and going.

Several minutes later, the busy, curly-haired hostess smiled and said, "Hi - How many? Two?"

"Yes, two, and we'd like a booth if there's one available."

She said, "There's a party getting up right over here. Follow me. We'll get the table cleaned off."

Walking past tables full of people eating, laughing and talking, Julie Hughes spotted her ex-boss and walked over to greet him and his wife while the hostess was seating Jeff. Julie came back over and sat down in the booth with Jeff moments later.

"Every time we come in here, we see somebody we know," she said.

"What are they doing?"

She said, "Craig told his wife that it was a night out of the kitchen - where did she want to go? The Drake Diner." A cute waitress walked up with glasses of water and menus.

She said "Hi, I'm Lisa." Julie told her that they already knew what they wanted. Lisa said, "Great."

Julie said, "I'd like a 'Maytag Blue Cheese Burger' and curly fries."

"What to drink?"

"Chocolate malt."

"And you?"

Jeff ordered a hot beef sandwich and an Anchor Steam beer. Lisa smiled and said she'd be right back.

"So Bill Clinton did it. I'm glad. What day's the inauguration?" Jeff asked.

"January 20th, I think. I hope he does as good as he looks." Julie replied. Jeff frowned and reminded her that there was more to running the country than looking good. She smiled and said that looking good was a good start. Lisa brought their order over and set it in front of them.

"Oh, it looks good. Thank you."

Lisa smiled and told them that if they needed anything to

just holler. The food was very good as usual. The malt was filling and the beer was cold. They were finishing the last bites when Lisa brought the bill over and said that they could pay at the counter. Julie thanked her and she walked away.

"Leave her a tip."

"I am."

As Jeff looked up toward the entrance, he saw a man in a coat making his way through the waiting patrons and moving behind the hostess at the cash register. He grabbed the hostess by the shoulder, she turned, and he put a handgun to her head. The man immediately fired, sending a bullet crashing through the young woman's skull. It showered the area with blood. The sound of the gunshot was deafening. She collapsed immediately, fatally wounded. People were screaming and ducking for cover. Jeff Hughes forcibly pushed his wife into a booth and shoved her to the floor. He fell in the booth behind her. A second loud shot rang out. There was momentary silence and people started screaming again. Smoke and the smell of cordite from the gun firing enveloped the area of the cash register.

Jeff heard one of the waitresses scream, "Oh my God! Oh my God! He's killed our managers! Oh my God! Don't kill me!" Someone screamed, "He shot her in the head! Somebody help her!" Jeff didn't see the gunman leave the restaurant. When he looked up, he saw that some customers were huddled, shivering and crying. Others ran out of the exits. Two diners were sprawled on the floor, covering their heads with their hands. Blood dripped down the east wall. Blood was everywhere in the area of the cash register and the bar. People were screaming, "Call the police! Oh my God! Call the police!" Jeff Hughes' ears were ringing from the gunshots.

Julie Hughes got up shaking. She looked over toward the cash register; the hostess who had been so nice to them when they arrived was lying behind the stand, mortally wounded. Blood covered the area. Julie started sobbing and bawling out loud. Jeff looked over at the two bodies on the floor – the hostess, and now a man as well. He was in a huge pool of his own blood. Both were obviously beyond any help. Traumatized witnesses were everywhere. They were outside the diner standing in groups. Some people who were approaching the entrance to the building when the shots rang out scrambled and hid between parked cars. Drake basketball players were entering the diner, unaware of what had just occurred. The gunman slipped past them making his escape. They stood dumbfounded, witnesses to the initial aftermath of homicide. A woman with two children had been in the booth closest to the door and witnessed the gruesome scene up close. The kids clutched her and sobbed uncontrollably. The woman huddled them close and had an expression of indescribable terror on her face. She couldn't even speak to comfort them or reassure them. A man was yelling for people to stay where they were and wait for the police. He yelled, "Please, please, anyone who saw the robber – anyone who saw anything please stay where you are! The robber is gone. The police will be here any minute!"

FRANTIC CALLER (actual calls): "Somebody please come to the Drake Diner right away. Please, please."
Police dispatcher: "What's the problem there?"
Caller: "We just got robbed. The manager has been shot!"
         (Moments later)
Police: "You just got robbed?"
Caller: "Yes."
Police: "Do you have any information about the person that robbed you?"
Caller: "He had a gun!"
Police: "OK. Wait a minute. Calm down so I can get the information, OK?"
Caller: "Oh my God! Oh my God!"
Police: "Ma'am, what's going on there?"
Caller: "They just killed our managers!"
Police: "Is the guy still there in the diner?"

Caller: "No! He left! He left!"

Police: "Ma'am, try to give me a description so we can catch this guy, OK?"

Caller: "I don't know!"

Police: "Is there somebody there that can tell me?"

Caller: "Oh my God! Did anybody see it? Oh my God!"

Police: "Ma'am, we're on our way, OK?"

Caller (crying): "Please help me! Hurry and get here please!"

Police: "Ma'am, can you hear me?"

Caller: "Yes!"

Police: "OK, we have police on the way, OK?"

Caller: "OK, I think he was black!"

Police: "You think he was black?"

Caller: "I think he had a green coat on!"

Police: "Black and he had a green coat?"

(Disconnect)

2ND CALLER –

Caller: "Drake Diner! We need an ambulance! Two people have been shot!"

3RD CALLER –

Caller: "The Drake Diner is being robbed!"

Police: "Are you there now?"

Caller: "No!"

Police: "Where are you now?"

Caller: "They're firing guns at the Drake Diner! I'm at the Zander's Café. I have a girl who just came from there!" [1]

DES MOINES POLICE UNITS arrived at the scene quickly. Patrolman Charlie Tedesco was one of the first to arrive. He rushed into the crime scene with his gun drawn, looked around at the situation and the carnage, and saw two children on the floor in a fetal position crying out loud. Other armed officers were now entering the diner. Charlie holstered his weapon, got down on the floor, and reassured the children that he was a policeman and everything was going to be all right. They both reached out for him and huddled in his arms shaking. The wail of sirens cut through the blustery night air from every direction as police and fire rescue units approached the scene. Within fifteen minutes, television crews were beginning to broadcast live from the scene. The crowds increased in size quickly - as did the number of police officers. It was a frigid Sunday night and, up until that point, a very uneventful night following the Thanksgiving weekend. Other police units left their assigned territories and moved into the general area of the diner, responding to radio calls with early descriptions of a suspect.

As news of the violence quickly spread, concerned family members and friends of the diner employees hurried to the scene. Names of the victims were not being released to the media. Employee family members had quickly arrived and were becoming impatient for news. Uniformed police were setting up a yellow tape, crime-scene perimeter surrounding the diner. The Polk County Medical Examiner, Dr. R.C. Wooters, pulled up in his white Cadillac with its red roof-mounted light-bar flashing. He was immediately hurried into the crime scene by officers.

Dr. Wooters walked over and stood over the dead hostess' body. He knelt for a closer look at the damage to her head. Her face was twisted and disfigured from the force of the point-blank shooting. Dr. Wooters' solemn expression gave some indication of his disgust with this sad situation. He stood up slowly and moved over to the other body. Detective Lieutenant Clarence Jobe explained to him how it appeared this had taken place. Jobe told him that the dead woman was Cara McGrane and the man was Harry Burnett, known as Tim Burnett – both were employees. He said she was shot for no reason or provocation that could be determined at that point and Burnett tried to stop it, and was shot in the face. One of the uniformed officers walked up to Dr. Wooters and quietly said to him that they thought they had a close relative of one of the victims outside.

Dr. Wooters turned, nodded his head and the two walked outside. The officer directed Wooters over to the yellow police line where three women were standing, shivering in the cold drizzle. The older woman identified herself as Phyllis Burnett and said, "Tim is my son. Did he die?" Always empathetic with violent crime victim's families, Dr. Wooters said softly that, yes, he was dead. She let out a moaning cry and nearly collapsed. She was escorted slowly through the crowd toward the building, supported by her two daughters, Charlene and Paulette.

DETECTIVE JIM ROWLEY was returning home from a weekend with his wife in Kansas City. It was an uneventful trip, very relaxing except for the lousy driving weather. As they turned on their street and approached the driveway he saw his daughter standing in front of the house. She looked anxious, waiting for them to pull in the driveway. "Dad, they've been calling for you every half hour. They need you over at the Drake Diner. There's been a double murder! It's already on TV - breaking news – on all the stations. Its bad!"

Jim ran in the house, called dispatch, retrieved his gun, and went to the diner. He turned onto 25th Street approaching the scene and he could tell from a distance that they had a major case on their hands. A large crowd was gathered outside the diner, police cars were all over the area and flashing red strobes lit the night. The media was already on the scene in force. Jim got out of his car and approached his supervisor, Lt. Jobe, outside the building. "What happened?" Jim asked.

Jobe turned to him, looked him up and down, and said, "Where have you been? What's with the cowboy hat? You been at a rodeo? We've been trying to find you."

"I just pulled in from Kansas City. My daughter said to get over here." Jobe said, "Double homicide. Robbery and the two managers shot to death. It's a mess inside."

Jim Rowley walked through the yellow crime-scene tape and entered the diner through the front doors. Jim was a large man with a charged and infectious voice that usually took over whatever space he was occupying. Veteran Lt. Jim Trotter, Identification Unit Commander, was standing near the booths inside, raising his eyebrows when he finally spotted Rowley. The area had the rust-like smell of human blood mixed with the smell of diner food – bad air. The distinguishable odor of blood was an old companion to Jim Rowley – the distinct stench of death. Jim had experienced this many, many times. The experienced homicide investigator knew this primordial stink from so many investigations.

Jim Rowley said, "Jim, tell me what we've got."

"We've got a mess on our hands is what we've got." Jim Trotter quickly explained what went down. He said, "Look around and take note, we want you to do one of your initial crime scene sketches that we all love, I'll walk you through the crime scene for the details." Trotter then accompanied him through the crime scene: two bodies lying near the cash register; blood and tissue splattered through the immediate surrounding area; many empty hurriedly abandoned tables. The female victim was slumped behind the cash register stand. The male victim had finally fallen a couple of feet away. Both suffered massive head wounds. Near the adjacent jukebox, Lt. Trotter pointed to an empty shell casing on the floor. "A .44 Magnum round with ejector marks on the casing." Rowley said he didn't know of a gun made that would fire a .44 round and then automatically eject it. Trotter looked at him and said, "I don't think I do either." Rowley turned and looked around and shook his head. A homicide investigation professional, Rowley was unusually taken aback by the conditions of the victims from just two shots. A .44 caliber bullet is capable of inflicting tremendous damage.

"What happened over here?" Rowley said, pointing to collapsed shelving.

Trotter said, "Victim #1, Cara McGrane's father has been in the crime scene already. McGrane's father is a state assistant attorney general. He went to the front door and flashed an AG badge (Attorney General) and our people wouldn't let him in. He came around and came in through the back door. He started charging in here screaming, 'It's my daughter in there!' He got far enough that I'm pretty sure he got a glimpse of his daughter's body on the floor. He went crazy. Jobe had to physically push him back and Jobe actually slammed him into that shelving that broke. Jobe was hollering, 'You don't want to see her like that!' He was moaning, bawling and screaming. It freaked some of the witnesses out. It was ugly."

"How'd he get here so fast?"

"He lives close. I told you - it's a fucked up mess! Plus, the Drake basketball team was in here when it happened and they tore out of here every which way. The shooter opens up and we've got black guys running out of the scene in every direction. We've got blood tracked through here by witnesses trying to escape. Plus, half the Des Moines Police Department has been in here."

Detective Rowley shook his head and said, "Another evidence nightmare." Uniformed officers walked over to Trotter and asked him what to do with the customer's jackets, gloves and handbags left in the booths as they ran out. Trotter calmly said to turn them over to the property section to be reclaimed later.

Trotter said that detective crews were taking witnesses to the station downtown for interviews and statements. Drake's basketball team ate at the diner through arrangements with the school while Drake was on Thanksgiving break. He didn't know how many witnesses had escaped the gunfire out of the various exits during and following the shots. "B-team, detective night crew, have some diner employees back in the kitchen taking statements."

All at once Rowley raised holy hell, "Huh-uh! No way! This is gonna be done right! This place needs to get locked down now! Everybody else out! Now!" He went back to the kitchen, told the nightshift detective to pack up, and told the witnesses in a softened voice to please sit tight.

Trotter and Rowley then walked slowly around the inside of the diner. Trotter said, "Some diner employee told the customers to clear out shortly after the shooting. But apparently one of the eyewitnesses made other witnesses stick around for us though. Thank God for cool heads."

The area around the cash register was now ominously quiet. Echoes of this crime shouted out to these experienced investigators. Cara McGrane was clad in a dark top, short black skirt, black panty hose – her face was disfigured in death; Tim Burnett's blood covered the area. Part of his skull and bunches of hair rested on a counter behind where he was shot. Jim Rowley, veteran crime scene unraveler, was putting a mental image of the crime together. People had trampled through the crime scene prior to the arrival of police. He worried that the loss of critical evidence might become irreplaceable in days and weeks ahead.

Trotter said, "I've also got the employee station map to copy that the waitresses use with table assignments. We can use these to figure out who was sitting where. We need to copy it and get them to all the teams interviewing. McDermott is setting up over here at the north end of the diner at the tables. He'll collect all the evidence once it's been noted, photographed and bagged. Bishop and Smith are photographing the scene. They're shooting all the evidence; the shell casings, bone fragments from the victims, both victims themselves. In fact, I want good close-ups of the victim's heads and wounds before they are moved. Bishop is sketching the eating area, counter areas and the bar for reference." Rowley said that he would further diagram the scene following Ident's (Identification Unit) completion of evidence gathering at the scene.

Drake Diner Director Steve Vilmain had arrived at the crime scene within minutes of the crime. He demanded entry and was finally allowed inside by Lt. Doug Nichols. Investigators securing the crime scene exchanged angry words about allowing *anyone* inside during this critical time of the initial investigation and evidence gathering. The diner owner, real estate mogul Bill Knapp, accompanied by Iowa Attorney General Bonnie Campbell and her husband, Ed Campbell, showed up and were very reluctantly allowed inside the crime scene as well. Drake University President Michael Ferrari was the final "civilian" allowed inside. Preservation of evidence was paramount.

Lt. Jobe told Sgt. Bob Ervin to head for the station and prepare for witness interviews. Some of the witnesses who were close to the shooting were transported to the downtown station by detectives. Crews would compare information gleaned from separated eyewitnesses to identify common descriptions of the perpetrator. Witness recollections were "all over the board" according to one initial investigator: The shooter was 5' 7" to 6' 1" and had a purple coat and a stocking cap. Someone else said he had a black parka with a hood. Another witness was certain he had on a green jacket and he had goggles. A Des Moines fireman who was a witness said he had glasses. Others said he had no glasses. Was he wild eyed and cocky, or was he calm as another woman remembered? People near the door heard him mention the Welcome Back sign by the door. Common threads: he was young, black, some witnesses close up said he had a gap between his front teeth, and several heard him say 'Merry Christmas' as he escaped through the door following the killings.

Rowley interviewed Mark Dilsaver, another manager of the Drake Diner, about how much money had been stolen. Dilsaver said they would have to figure that out. He said he had no idea at that point how many unpaid bills there were as a result of patrons scrambling out of the diner. Rowley questioned Dilsaver about whether he personally had any suspects in mind or whether he had any disgruntled employees. He stated that he had one disgruntled employee who was fired for tardiness and not showing up for work. But Dilsaver said that he was a high school student and he wouldn't consider him a suspect.

Reconstruction of the crime scene consisted of determining where the customer witnesses were seated, the direction they were facing, who they were there with, and what they saw. One problem with witness interviewing is that eyewitnesses often talk to each other immediately following the crime. Witnesses will add someone else's recollection to their own trying to be helpful. In that fashion, inaccurate information reported by a number of witnesses can become a problem. The complexity of this particular crime scene was a test of forensic knowledge, experience and expertise of all the forensic and criminal investigators involved.

WITNESS INTERVIEWS were top priority immediately following the initial investigation at the crime scene as well as at the detective bureau on third floor "cop-shop" downtown. Detectives interviewed Thomas E. Nelson and his wife, Cindy Meek. These interviews were conducted shortly after the crime in order to draw upon recollections fresh in their minds.

Mr. Nelson related that he arrived separately from his wife, her mother and their two nieces – in fact, there were nine people in their party waiting to be seated. They were standing in front of the hostess stand/cash register and Cindy Meek was standing with two children next to the jukebox that stood directly north of the hostess stand. They observed the killer as he maneuvered through the crowd: they said he came up behind Cara McGrane and shot her in the head immediately. Cindy Meek instantaneously pulled the children toward the front doors. Cindy was wearing black denim jeans and she reported an instant sharp pain in her upper right thigh following the first gunshot. Her husband, Tom, hustled the rest of their family out of the diner's front doors. He said he actually heard the second shot before he could get everyone safely out of the diner.

Jan Jensen, the assistant coach of the Drake University Women's Basketball Team and her friend, Jay Hatch, entered the Drake Diner a little before 7:00 p.m.. There were several people standing around the entrance waiting to be seated. They asked Cara McGrane if they could sit at the counter at the south end of the diner. There were two empty stools there. Cara smiled and said, "Of course." As soon as they walked over and were seated they saw the killer move around and shoot her. Jay Hatch pushed Jan to the floor and they both heard the second shot. Jan recalled that she heard the killer say "nobody move!" She said he was black, wearing a gray stocking cap and a dark blue parka with full hood. He was holding a black gun that appeared to be an automatic. According to her, he was holding it with both hands when he shot her. Jensen and Hatch looked up and saw him running south from the diner.

Lisa Deaton and Leslie Gerhart were sitting at a table toward the north end of the diner. They both heard the first gunshot. Leslie stood up and saw smoke surrounding the cash register - she crouched down immediately. They began crawling farther to the north when they heard the second round fired. They heard the employees start screaming; Lisa and Leslie got up, looked around, saw the bodies and ran out of the north emergency door.

Cindy Meek's black jeans were covered with Cara McGrane's blood. Fragments from the bullet that killed her were imbedded in the fabric of the jeans. Cindy went home to change clothes before they came to the police station. She had a large black bruise from the shooting on her upper right thigh. She brought the black jeans with her to the police station and Detective Rowley put them into evidence. Tom Nelson was loaned a Polaroid by police to take pictures of the bruise on his wife's thigh for evidence. She was listed as "Victim #3". Their descriptions of the killer were very similar to the other witnesses who had a close look at him.

Detectives interviewed a lady named Jodie Guill. Ms. Guill said she was driving down University Avenue and at 7:01 p.m., a black male, approximately 5'10" tall and 150 pounds ran right in front of her car at 24th and University. He was running north and didn't look either way as he ran across University. She stated that he looked right at her as he nearly collided with her car. She got a very good look at him and she said that she could identify him. He was wearing a big athletic coat with an LA Raiders emblem on the back and he was wearing a gray stocking cap. She said, "I was face to face. I almost hit him. There's no doubt in my mind I can identify him."

Most of the initial call-in leads that came in from the immediate vicinity of the murders related a black man running from the Drake Diner. With the Drake basketball team scattering following the incident, most of these turned out to be of no real value to the investigation. Following later interviews with the Drake players, detectives were able to match up individual neighborhood eye-witness reports of "a black man running" with the paths of exit from the scene reported by many of the Drake basketball players trying to escape the gunfire and carnage.

Rowley and Detective Rick Singleton were assigned follow-up on lead number 26 – Carl Soderlund, 2717 Carpenter. They interviewed him at his fiancé's apartment. He and his fiancé, Jennifer Pelton, had just walked into the diner when the first shot was fired. He said that he was in the entryway and saw the suspect shoot Cara McGrane in the head. He said the suspect was holding the gun in his right hand and it looked like a large semi-automatic with a dark finish, but it did not look like normal bluing on the weapon. The suspect did not look straight at him but he did see the suspect's face and hands. He was not wearing gloves. After hearing the first shot, Soderlund and his fiancé ran out the front door and were running north when they heard the second shot fired. Soderlund said he looked back and saw people running out of the diner in every direction. He and his fiancé ran to Zander's Café and told the staff there to call 911. Detective Singleton asked him if he saw the suspect exit the scene and he said he did not. He asked him if he could ID the suspect and he wasn't sure. Soderlund's description of the suspect was a black male wearing a dark blue three quarter length parka with the hood up. When he first saw him, he was wearing a gray mask with eyeholes and mouth hole cut out, but Soderlund said he did lift it exposing his face.

Jennifer Pelton's statement was pretty much the same since they were together, but demonstrating that different people see different things, there were some discrepancies. She said that they walked up to the diner and saw that it was crowded with lots of congestion around the doorway. As they entered the diner she met two people she recognized as Drake basketball players, Adrian Thomas and Rudy Washington, Jr.'s roommate whom she only knew as "Khary." She said she had just glanced down as she was maneuvering around the people when she heard the first shot. She looked up, saw the suspect behind the counter holding the gun with both hands and pointing it at a downward angle. She thought he shot the cash register and she remembered seeing lots of smoke. She did not see a mask on the suspect and her description coincided with Soderlund's. She said that as they were running away she heard the second shot and people screaming. She said she was scared to death at that moment. Rowley asked her if she could ID him and she thought she could if she was confronted with him.

Patrol Sergeant Dave Murillo was the first "gold-braid" (police sergeant or higher in rank) to respond to and arrive at the crime scene. Murillo said, "I was at 28th and Ingersoll working 502 as west-side sergeant that night. I was working a domestic call. Dispatch came on the air for all west-side cars to head for the Drake Diner – two persons shot, shooter may still be at the scene. I was a mile away and started that direction light and siren. Then I suddenly remembered that I'd responded to a car accident trip as soon as I got to my black-and-white after roll call and hadn't loaded my shotgun yet. I'm racing to the diner, driving with my knee on the steering wheel, loading the shotgun - hoping the shooter hadn't got away. I pulled up to the scene, made my way through the crowd that was gathering and I went in with my officers. In my experience, it was one of the most gruesome scenes I've ever been involved in as a police officer. Both victims were shot in the head at close range with a powerful handgun. From an evidence-gathering standpoint, fleeing witnesses and diner employees had already trampled through the crime scene. I've never seen anything like this."

Des Moines Police Detective Jim Rowley

Chapter Two

MONDAY, NOVEMBER 30th did *not* start off like any other day at the Des Moines Police Department. Newspaper headlines announced "2 are slain at Drake Diner – Robber shoots while patrons dive for cover." A photo of victim Tim Burnett's mother being helped from the scene of her murdered son reinforced the personal tragedy of this crime. Early morning TV news broadcasts were exclusive to the Drake Diner tragedy.

News crews and reporters blanketed the police station at East First and Court searching for any report or interview they could find. As senior officers arrived at work, the reporters chased them looking for a break. National wire services picked up the story. Minneapolis, Omaha and Kansas City news services carried stories documenting the tragedy.

Des Moines Police Assistant Chief of Criminal Investigation Bill McCarthy immediately called a morning briefing for assigned investigators and staff. Twenty-four detectives and many additional subordinates were in attendance. The Department pulled in officers from other divisions and units to bolster the number of sworn personnel involved. McCarthy began with an initial statement of the situation. He said, "I know that some of you have been up all night and it goes with the job. We have a major case on our hands. My phone hasn't stopped ringing. As you already know, we have two dead managers of the Drake Diner. They were shot pointblank while the place was open and full of customers. As far as we can determine, approximately fifty people were in the diner when this occurred. We have eyewitnesses but we also have a variety of descriptions of the shooter. What we do know is that he is a young, black male, approximately six feet tall, wearing a dark sweatshirt, coat and dark trousers. The handgun used is important. According to Jim Trotter, it's a .44 Magnum semi-automatic – unusual gun. It made one hell of a mess – massive head wounds – both killed instantly. The diner is closed down. Ident is still over there." Then he pointed to firearms expert Detective Warren Martin, "Martin, I want you to concentrate on this gun that he used." Martin nodded his acknowledgement.

McCarthy continued, "Gentlemen, this is a top priority matter. We are assigning eight two-man teams to start following up leads. We have seating charts of the diner. We are figuring out where each witness was seated, the direction that they were facing, and what they saw. Members of the Drake basketball team were eating there when it happened. We will need to coordinate interviewing those people. Patrol will be assisting with the neighborhood, crowd control, and other assignments as we see fit. Patrol *will not* talk to the press. And, I think it's important that this office be careful with what is said or otherwise communicated in any way. The media has gone into meltdown already. There will be an avalanche of coverage. This whole thing is a political bombshell. Chief Moulder wants results. We are already saturated with leads. All the people dying to cooperate with us will be calling in. We need to separate solid leads from the trash. State DCI has offered their help with both investigators and their lab. The suburbs and the county will assist. Unless I'm wrong, we are going to need every bit of help we can muster. Bob Ervin will pass out the two-man team assignments and start handing out leads. I want the leads handled properly. We know that the junk leads are pouring in. But, somewhere in those, there may be an important tip - a new lead that could break this case. We're going to have detectives reassigned from property to handle a phone line that we're setting up. We need to segregate and channel all calls concerning this crime. I also realize the pending workload that you guys currently have. We're just going to have to do the best we can with what we've got."

The meeting adjourned promptly. Detective Rowley was assigned to work with Detective Rick Singleton, who was transferred from arson investigation for this case. The two detectives had worked together previously on homicides and they had good personal chemistry. Rick was a thirteen-year veteran who had been a detective for four years. They worked together the night of the shooting, conducting an interview in the station with Jonas Chladek, a tenth grade student at Dowling High School who worked part time at the diner. Jonas had worked Sunday until about two-thirty in the afternoon, but he couldn't pick up his tips for the day until later on. His mother drove him over to the diner from their home on Pleasant Street about 6:45 p.m. Jonas followed the soon-to-be killer into the diner, witnessed him work his way around behind Cara McGrane, and was standing about four feet away when the killer shot her in the head. Jonas instinctively turned and ran out the southeast door of the kitchen as he heard the second shot. He saw the suspect run from the building. He thought he would be able to identify the killer.

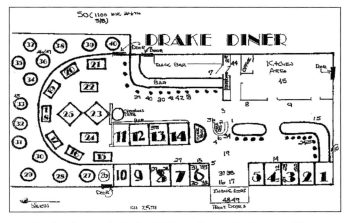

Seating diagram indicating table numbers and witness positions.

LT. CLARENCE "LADDIE" JOBE, unit commander of the 'Crimes Against Persons' section, continued with a combined investigative team including members of other area departments for an additional update briefing: "Here's how the whole thing went down as far as we can determine at this point: We've got a suspect, black, approximately 5'8" to 6' tall, thin, believed to be young but no age has been agreed on yet, wearing a long, black three quarter length coat with hood, the hood up, possibly with a sports logo, Raiders or something on the back. In addition, he was wearing a stocking cap, maybe gray – pulled down as he entered the establishment – but he pulled it up to reveal his facial features during the commission of the crime. He may have had on an additional nylon stocking or cap on under the other stocking cap. He wore no gloves but there appears to be no latent prints left by the suspect at the scene. He was armed with a black .44 Magnum semi-automatic, a large weapon that may have had silver on the side of the weapon and reportedly possibly had a luminescent 'red dot' sight on it reported by witnesses."

"There were fifty to sixty people in the restaurant at the time. There were probably fifteen people in the entrance, in the area of the cash register, waiting to be seated. The entry way was congested and the doorway was semi-blocked due to the crowd waiting and the lousy weather conditions outside – drizzle and rain. Had the weather been nicer, all of these people probably wouldn't have been jammed in the entryway."

"We have assembled the following scenarios from the statements of witnesses so far–witnesses at various stages of the incident and various locations in relation to the incident. I will refer to the witness by number, which you all can refer to on the witness list and sheets in front of you and on the diner diagram up front here. Witness #5 was behind the suspect as he entered the establishment. The suspect opened the door and allowed two women to exit the diner. He bumped into Witness #11, a Drake basketball player, and exchanged words with Witness #11 who related that the suspect had a stocking cap pulled down over his full face as he entered the building, but that he pulled it up as he entered. Both witnesses #5 and #11 report that at that time, the suspect raised the .44 magnum and was holding it in this right hand. According to them, he made no attempt to conceal it at all."

"At this moment, victim Cara McGrane was returning to the rear of the horseshoe-shaped cash register counter. The suspect maneuvered through the crowd around the entrance, dropped the .44 Magnum to his side about that time, moved around the right side of the cash register area, and approached victim McGrane from the same side. He grabbed her right shoulder from behind with his left hand."

"Reports so far of the verbal exchange were: Witness #21 remembers hearing the suspect say, 'Give me the money, bitch!' at which time she brushed her hair back and turned, thinking it was a joke. Witness #43 remembers her turning and saying, 'What do you want?' Anyhow, whatever was actually said, when she turned her head, he put the .44 Magnum against her right jaw, pointblank, and fired one round. Victim McGrane collapsed behind the cash register, fatally wounded. Witnesses report that the suspect began rifling the cash register and he said, 'Don't anybody move!' Several witnesses heard that. Manager Tim Burnett, who was off-duty that night, but there decorating a Christmas tree with his wife, Mary Beth, on hearing the shot, pushed his wife onto the north patio for protection. He ran to the assistance of Cara McGrane. The suspect saw him coming and met him, left hand full of cash. He shot him with the .44 Magnum, in a downward motion through the left jaw from close range. Tim Burnett collapsed on the floor on his left side, fatally wounded as well. By that time people were screaming and taking cover, some were exiting the diner through the four exits. The suspect escaped through the front door, dropping bills as he went, hollering 'Merry Christmas.' He ran to the south, went around the building, and then he ran north from the crime scene.

One of the witnesses started chasing him but came back to keep witnesses at the scene until we arrived. A male employee of the Drake Diner told everyone to 'clear the restaurant immediately – the restaurant is closed."

CARA MCGRANE was popular with everyone. She was a naturally outgoing young woman who truly enjoyed working at the diner. She graduated from Hoover High School in Des Moines and studied theater at the University of Northern Iowa. She was one of the original staff at The Drake Diner and was characterized by her boss, Steve Vilmain, as "drop dead gorgeous." She had left The Drake Diner to manage The West End Diner and had just returned to "her home" as she described it, The Drake Diner, when the tragedy occurred. She wanted to use the money she earned working to attend classes at Drake University. She loved the neighborhood and used to go to the old Varsity Theatre, across from Drake, and watch film noir classics from the 1940's and '50's.

People said that they had never seen her in a bad mood. She loved to joke and had the nickname "Chicken-legs." According to her friend Marci Christensen, she socialized with a large circle of friends and with her family. She lived at home in nearby Beaverdale with her parents, two sisters Molly and Gillian, and brother Toll. Her father, Tom, was lawyer for the Iowa Board of Parole and an Iowa Assistant Attorney General. Her mother, Jo McGrane, was a staff member on the Iowa Board of Parole. "Her sisters," Christensen said, "were her best friends. Anytime we would go out, whether it was to the mall or a movie, or a bar or whatever, Cara would know someone. She had great friends and a great laugh. It was loud and it was great." [2]

Tim and Lyle Burnett were identical twins born in that order nineteen minutes apart on June 12th, 1964. Harry Timothy and Lyle Kimberly were the youngest of Phyllis Burnett's six children. Prior to raising a family, Phyllis had been a circus performer and member of a three-tier, high-wire act that had performed for audiences ranging from the Iowa State Fair to the Emperor of Japan. Tim and Lyle's sister, Paulette Sandstrom, remembered how close the two boys were. "The boys were inseparable. After high school when Lyle joined the Marines and moved to California, I saw the effects on Tim. You could just tell he was a lost soul when Lyle was gone. And then when Lyle moved to Phoenix, you could see it all over again."

They lived apart four of their twenty-eight years. They dressed alike as children confusing their teachers. They went into the restaurant business together as teenagers at Uncle Jack's Tacos. Tim worked at different establishments later on including The DuckBlind where, as a manager, he met his future wife Mary. Friends say the two hit it right off. Tim made her a part of all the activities he enjoyed – wind surfing, hang gliding, scuba diving and golf. Tim was especially proud of the hole-in-one that he shot at Waveland Golf Course.

Tim was an original member of the staff that opened The Drake Diner in 1987. Later, he and Mary followed an opportunity offered to him and moved to Arizona where Tim managed a trendy restaurant. But Mary wanted to move back to Des Moines after about a year and Tim agreed. Steve Vilmain offered him his job back at The Drake Diner as the new general manager - Tim accepted. On the evening of Sunday, November 29th, 1992, Tim was off but wanted to set up and decorate a Christmas tree at work for employees and customers to enjoy. Mary agreed to come in and help him. She liked decorating Christmas trees – Christmastime was such a special time of year for them.

Bill McCarthy went into Chief Bill Moulder's office and closed the door. Chief Moulder was used to upper echelon police personnel coming into his office with promises and ambitious declarations. McCarthy's message was the opposite and sobering. Moulder's face was expressionless, awaiting what McCarthy had to say that required closing the door. He slowly said, "We've got nothing - except a description that could fit ten thousand people. This is going to tax our manpower to the limit. I could use fifty more investigators right now and unless we turn a corner quick, this could be a long, long haul."

Chief Moulder sat back slowly in his chair, crossed his arms and said, "If the killer is from out of town, out of state and already gone . . ." McCarthy stopped him mid-sentence and said he didn't think that was the case and hoped to God Moulder wasn't right.

FOLLOWING THE DRAKE DINER MURDERS outraged reactions spun out of control; tips and leads poured into the police department; community leaders began work to rebuild confidence in the Drake neighborhood. The Des Moines Police held a televised news conference on Monday morning, November 30th. Lt. Jobe was department spokesman for the criminal investigation. In a serious tone, he told the audience of restless reporters and officials that he would only detail facts of the crime and give a description of the suspect. He was reluctant to field a lot of questions at that time, but he was obliged to answer some relating to the suspect if it would help to solve this quickly. Reporters asked if they had a specific suspect at this point. Jobe said, "No, we do not." They asked if information was coming in. Jobe said, "Yes." Reporters asked if it was a grudge against the diner. Jobe answered, "I have no comment," and he concluded the questioning at that point.

Jim Rowley and Detective Richard Singleton were effective working together. Also assigned to the case were detectives Dennis Westover, Ron Bjornson, Ralph Roth and sixteen others. Detectives and ancillary personnel were taken from other units and reassigned to The Drake Diner case – case number 92-51577. Detectives William Boggs and Steve Mickelson, as well as Singleton, were reassigned from the property section to this investigation. Other property and special assignment detectives were assigned to handle existing "persons" cases. The announcement of the possible murder weapon used, a

Desert Eagle .44 Magnum automatic, resulted in owners of that particular handgun bringing their guns to police headquarters or calling in. Police ballistics expert, Detective Warren Martin, addressed the media, inadvertently referred to the Desert Eagle as "the world's most 'powerfullest' handgun." The press picked right up on that. He also told them that the weapon was three times as powerful as a nine millimeter. Results of the eyewitness interviews were being pieced together. Two young children who saw the shooter brought crayons with them from the diner to police headquarters. They sketched the killer as a huge, scary monster.

A media firestorm had begun. Veteran officers often said that the media goes through an unusual drill in these type of cases: They scream 'Catch them! Catch them!' Until we catch them, they accuse us of being incompetent. When we finally catch them, we're accused of police brutality. Then, before we can get them to trial, the media gives them trial-by-media. And then, when we get them convicted, the media wants them saved by trying to prove they were insane in the first place! And they wonder why we feel the way we do sometimes.

The media extensively covered an afternoon news conference with community leaders, including Governor Terry Branstad; Des Moines Police Chief Bill Moulder; Iowa Attorney General Bonnie Campbell; Drake University President Michael Ferrari; Drake Diner Owner (and Drake Board of Trustees Member) Bill Knapp; and Larry Carter, local Executive Director of the NAACP. They denounced the deplorable crime, spoke of the effort to bring the killer to justice and asked for the community's cooperation and calm. A $20,000 reward for information leading to the killer, sponsored by The City of Des Moines and Polk County Crime Stoppers, was formally announced.

While the community leaders asked for cooperation and calm, the media launched into stories about how dangerous the Drake area actually was. A story characterized the diner neighborhood as one of the City's most dangerous neighborhoods based on a review of the former year's crime statistics (1991). The Drake Business Association countered that police foot patrols had been effective in the area for fourteen years. The media shot back with reports from Drake students saying that it wasn't safe to go east of the Drake campus. The press reported that area residents said they often heard gunshots.

In a story headlined "Diner neighbors find reason for fear," Drake student Deana Horas was quoted as saying "I'm very concerned about people coming to Drake now because, in my eyes, this is a very good reason for some people to be scared of the area." [3] Storeowner Harry Young told the media, "It's not the best place to have a business, but I will keep it here." Drake area business owners hoped that this tragedy would not ruin their businesses. Drake University was fielding calls from anxious Drake parents and family members. Some students were considering leaving Drake altogether as a result of the situation now being further complicated by adverse publicity such as the newspaper headline "Slayings rattle workers in Drake neighborhood." However, *The Des Moines Register* published editorials by people like journalist Craig Textor, objecting to the way the Register handled the coverage of the slayings.[4]

The atmosphere surrounding The Drake Diner murders and Drake University's close proximity to the murders was highly charged. Drake's offices were answering calls from Drake parents in New York, Connecticut, and Massachusetts. The negativity seemed at times overwhelming. Dr. Michael Ferrari was requesting additional police intervention to calm the nerves of students and their families. The advent in recent years of the extensive and widespread high-speed accessibility of breaking news had created a situation never before experienced in such a negative way by Drake University. The fact that the diner carried the name Drake seemed to fuel the fire even more.

Barry Howe and his wife, Michelle, lived in the Drake neighborhood. Barry had lived in the neighborhood since he was a child. Barry's father, Lawrence, taught biology at Drake and had settled the family in a large two-story home with a spacious front porch near 29th and Cottage Grove. Back then, a front porch on Cottage Grove was an invitation for people to stop and engage in friendly conversation. Many Drake University faculty members had residences in this charming area during that time. Later, in 1982, Barry and Michelle bought a home on 34th street, five blocks west of Drake. Michelle was more aware (or vocal) than Barry of increasing trouble in the Drake neighborhood. There had been muggings, sexual assaults and altercations that now, with changing times, involved more guns and increased violence. Michelle wanted to move west to West Des Moines, Clive or Urbandale where she would feel safer for Barry, their three children, and herself. The Drake Diner murders were "the last straw." A local TV news crew was gathering opinions about the murders from people outside Dahl's grocery store at 35th and Ingersoll. Michelle was asked if she lived in the area and what she thought. She thought for a moment that she was going to start crying. But she took a deep breath and told them that the Drake neighborhood was not what it used to be; wasn't safe to live in anymore and was being taken over by robbers, drug dealers and criminals who weren't afraid to kill someone for no reason. The six o'clock news ran her unedited comments. Barry was not happy with her blanket condemnation of the Drake area that had always been his home turf.

KEY INVESTIGATIVE personnel were called together in a stuffy third floor conference room around 6:00 p.m. Monday evening to discuss and brainstorm theories related to the crime. They included Chief of Detectives Bill McCarthy, Lt. Jobe, Lt. Jim Trotter, Sgt. Bob Ervin, Ralph Roth and several experienced detectives including Jim Rowley. Everyone was tired but the meeting was necessary and couldn't be postponed. Jobe opened the discussion by saying that they wanted everyone's ideas. All they could say for sure at that point was that the motive was robbery. Did the killer intend to shoot when he went in? Was there a lookout?

Ervin interjected that witnesses saw and chased only one suspect. Detective Dennis Westover said, "A lookout, an accomplice, could have easily faded into the crowd and escaped in the confusion following the crime." He continued, "If there was a lookout, did he know there was going to be a shooting?" Jobe said that *if* there was a lookout, and *if* the lookout was shocked and/or scared that murders had occurred, this person would be extremely important to find since he or she could be an accessory only and could "put the shooter away."

Sgt. Bob Ervin was a good seasoned cop - focused but high strung, very talented. He knew the importance of forging personal relationships and he devoted time to the people important to his law enforcement career and his personal life. He said, "The shooter ran to the south, around the building and ran back to the north between the buildings, chased by a witness for a short distance. No one we talked to who lives back there, including people who heard the commotion and looked out, remembers seeing a man getting into a waiting car. We've already canvassed the neighborhood."

Lt. Jobe squinted at Ervin, "Maybe the getaway car was farther away."

Bob shook his head, "I think the killer might live within a few blocks of the diner or has a safe house, maybe a gang house, to hide out in."

Chief McCarthy had learned a long time ago in police work the importance of addressing assumptions. He pursed his lips momentarily, nodded and said, "Interesting point - makes sense."

Jim Rowley stood up, walked over and closely examined the diagram of the interior of the diner that was pinned to a wall. He said, "The guy was cool, calm and collected during the whole deal. No raving psychopathic maniac here. And he shoots Cara McGrane right off the bat. We have to assume that she would have been the only victim if Burnett hadn't come to her aid." Ervin added that he would have shot anyone interfering or blocking his escape. Rowley sat back down and said, "Well, it's one for the books."

Westover offered, "Hate crime?"

Lt. Trotter leaned back in his chair, grimaced and added, "Young black man hates whites - suppose. Here's this beautiful white woman who won't give him the time of day – won't respond, she brushes him off. She's gleaming and smiles at the young, white guy - witness Scott Birrer - waiting to be seated and spontaneously the killer reacts to all the times he's been ignored - by killing her outright. I agree that *if* there was an accomplice, he or she did not expect this – two murders bringing all this coverage, all this outrage and all this heat down." Westover wondered out loud if the shooter had contact with Cara McGrane prior to the killing – revenge or payback or something. Everyone agreed that was doubtful as she didn't recognize or acknowledge him in any way according to the witnesses. This didn't seem to be anyone she would know.

Assistant Chief Bill McCarthy, with his extensive law enforcement experience and education says, "A textbook *misogynist* possibly."

Ralph Roth looked at McCarthy with a puzzled expression and said, "Misogynist."

McCarthy sat quietly for a moment and said, "The clinical misogynist hates women – here's a good looking woman, add if you want that she's white and she ignores him. But he hates all women, and the misogynist's condition usually includes violence against women. He came to rob but in this case he shoots her on sudden impulse. Then Tim Burnett charged him and he just reacted. The killer is out of control with the temporary power that the gun provides, he just shoots Cara McGrane – and then, unfortunately, Burnett too."

One suggestion was that the department should announce that they believe there was an accomplice and ask him or her to come forward and that they would possibly be granted immunity and maybe even a reward in return for his or her testimony.

Chief McCarthy shook his head and said they were not going to start down that path since it was based on conjecture, not hard evidence. McCarthy looked around and asked if anyone had any information from his interviews indicating a lookout or another suspicious person. Nobody did.

Rowley leaned way back in his chair, turned and looked at the diagram on the wall of the crime scene with the positions of the bodies outlined and an icon representing the shooter and lines indicating the travel of the bullets. Then he sat up straight in the chair, picked up and thumbed through the glossy ident photos taken at the scene – images of Cara McGrane's body prostrate on the bloody floor, close-ups of Tim Burnett's shattered skull, pictures of blood and brain matter on the walls. He laid the photos down and thought about how tired he was right at that moment. He went home following the meeting.

Jim Rowley arrived at home around 10:30 p.m. He went into their comfortable ranch-style home, didn't see his wife right off and walked into their bedroom. His wife, Connie, was lying in bed with the TV on. She was watching "Cheers", but turned the set off when Jim walked in. They exchanged greetings as Jim took off his gun and took his badge out of his coat pocket. He laid both on the dresser and just stood there for a moment. Connie was familiar with his moods at times like this and asked him if they were making any progress. He said, "I don't know. The image of the bodies is stuck in my mind. This is a bad one." Connie was thinking that she wanted Jim to join her in some early Christmas shopping for their family but she knew now that would be impossible.

DES MOINES POLICE Chief William Moulder assigned Detectives Rowley and Rick Singleton to go out to Drake and address a closed-door meeting of Drake University Administration and the Board of Trustees. President Ferrari, sitting at the end of the conference table, apologized to the detectives for having to call the meeting under those circumstances, but Drake, he said, was in a precarious position.

Rowley spoke in calm, general terms concerning the progress of the investigation. The lack of solid leads made the task of instilling much faith in these people all the more daunting. There was another problem that Drake actually had some control over: Several members of Drake's basketball team and some of their managers were witnesses to the murder. Detectives had not been allowed to interview these individuals. Drake's basketball coach Rudy Washington, Sr., who was black, seemed to be stonewalling the police department's efforts to gather whatever helpful information these athletes had. President Ferrari assured the detectives that there would be cooperation from the basketball team and staff.

State DCI criminal investigation liaison agent Doug Fagan was working with Des Moines Police coordinating state help and lending his personal law enforcement experience. He was a former state trooper who transferred to the criminal investigation division. Unfortunately, his "road experience" with the state patrol wasn't a lot of help in this instance. Agent Fagan told Jim Rowley that his *gut feeling* was that the Drake Diner was a gang-related crime. Rowley told him, "My only problem with that is once you get that *gut feeling,* Doug, the only things you will see are things that reinforce it." Rowley kept his personal conclusions at that point to himself. He felt robbery was the main objective - maybe a combination of robbery and the killer's hatred of white people. Nevertheless, he kept an open mind as to motive.

Each morning, detective crews thumbed through seven or eight new leads wondering if one would be the lucky hit. Most of the leads looked shallow – investigators were suspicious of the vague leads they were assigned. Everyone wanted to solve the case and get the credit. They were suspicious of "lead-stacking" that gave certain officers the best leads. Most leads were Crime Alert and Crime-Stopper stuff - a man was seen at 23rd and Forest wearing a Raider full length coat, high school kids telling their girlfriends that they knew who did it, an ex brother-in-law who was capable of just this sort of crime. They thought the "golden boys" of investigation would get the real hot leads on this. All that Sergeant Dave Murillo would say was that the offer of reward money makes these people that call in crazy – or crazier. He said, "Professionally, each of our officers would obviously like to be the hero on this. This is career building material."

Detectives Westover and Schultz received a tip that Derrick "Scooter" Davis, a black male, 25, approximately the right height, had been flashing money around that week. Checking with "Ident," Davis had a record for carrying a concealed weapon, assault and drug possession. He was listed as living at 1048 19th Street. Detectives paid a call to the residence. The lady that answered the door identified herself as Derrick's mother, Theresa Monroe. She asked the officers to come in and she told them that Derrick was in Chicago on Sunday night, the night of the murders. She was sure because she called and talked to him after the shootings were announced on the news. She was very cooperative and seemed angered as many in the black community were concerning this crime. The detectives marked the lead "no further follow-up at this time."

Detective Larry Bedford received a call from a reliable informant that someone who had information about the Drake Diner murders wanted to meet with him in the swimming pool parking lot across from North High School at 11:00 p.m. The party with information was supposedly afraid for his or her life. Bedford was home that evening but took a chance on a cold and rainy night. He got a back-up unit from tactical and went to the rendezvous. They stayed until 1:00 a.m. but nobody showed up.

Rowley and Singleton paid a visit to an attorney - Dennis Scemel. He was an avid gun collector and shooter. He owned a stainless steel .44 Desert Eagle that he bought from a gun dealer in Huxley, Iowa. Scemel told them that the .44 Desert Eagle that was being displayed on TV might not be the murder weapon.

The officers wanted to know why. He said the gun they were looking for could also be an L.A.R. Grizzly .44 Magnum, manufactured out west. He believed the Grizzly semi-automatic would also chamber any .44 Magnum round. Shooting enthusiast friends of his called the Grizzly the most powerful handgun they had ever seen.

Officer Larry Reynolds drew the lead to follow up with Dontrell Ducker. He was a senior at Roosevelt High School who worked at the Drake Diner and was present the night of the murders. Ducker said that he got a good look at the killer that seemed to freeze in his mind. Reynolds brought him to the police station to view the composite of the suspect. Ducker looked at the composite closely and made some changes – to include a large gap between his front teeth. Lt. Trotter looked at the finished composite for a long moment, and then ordered copies to be distributed to all officers involved in the investigation. He said later that Ducker was so sure of the killer's appearance that it charged up everyone in the room that day.

Detectives were handed a lead phoned in by a Jeff Johnson. He told them that a Mr. Hicks, who lived at 400 SE Diehl, owned a Desert Eagle and had sold it recently and he thought the police should find out why. They went to 400 SE Diehl and spoke with Frank Manders who lived there. He didn't know of anybody by the name of Hicks. As they were leaving, they noticed a plaque in front of 406 SE Diehl with the name Hicks on it.

They went to the door and knocked. The man who answered was Harry Hicks. They asked him about the report that he had a Desert Eagle and the circumstances surrounding it. He said that he had purchased a .44 Desert Eagle from the gunsmith at Floyd's Sporting Goods. He fired it one time and realized just how powerful a weapon it was. He ran an ad in the paper and sold the gun to Donnie Faber, Jr. Faber later told investigators that he bought the gun to give to his father. The gun was still in his father's possession.

Sgt. Bob Ervin took an anonymous phoned in lead – number 122. They named a Freddie C. Clark as a suspect. The lead was turned over to Jim Rowley to follow up. He found out that Clark lived at 2212 Carpenter and was a black 17-year-old juvenile. Clark had an arrest record including assault, carrying a concealed weapon, robbery and attempted murder. His nickname was "Alf." He lived with his mother and was thought to be a member of the Vice Lords gang. No further follow-up could be done since it was an anonymous call-in.

Sgt. Larry Cramer passed on a lead that he received from a Wayne Gaskill. Gaskill said that he saw a tall black man, wearing gray pants, a gray sweatshirt and a three quarter length dark NFL coat at the Seven-Eleven store at 22nd and University just prior to the murders at about 6:20 p.m. He was acting extremely nervous and Gaskill said he could identify the suspect.

Rick Singleton made contact with Mr. Gaskill. He said the man was on the pay phone in front of the store. The man got off the phone and was pacing back and forth in front of the store and up and down the west alley beside the store. Gaskill was pumping gas into his car at the gas island while making these observations. He noticed a young, white woman and another black man who was pushing a baby stroller walking to the front of the store. This black man left the baby stroller out in the parking lot and approached the first man and carried on a conversation.

Gaskill said that he walked into the store to pay for his gas and remarked to the attendant, Chris Bald, that it was strange for people to bring a young baby out on such a crummy night and just leave the baby in the parking lot exposed to the inclement weather. The attendant agreed and said that she had been watching that as well.

Detectives Westover and Bjornson arranged a photo spread to show Gaskill that contained a photo of Andre Jenkins, who was a current suspect. Rowley took the photo spread to Gaskill's place of work and showed him the display. He could not identify anyone in the spread.

Officers then showed Mr. Gaskill another photo spread that contained Jason Brown, an informant for Detectives Westover and Bjornson, who they had information was at the Seven-Eleven that night. They figured he was the black man pushing the baby stroller. Gaskill studied him carefully and said he just couldn't be sure at this time. Investigators had little choice but to close this particular lead for the time being.

Des Moines Police were now enlisting the help of a case management software program acquired from the FBI that had been used in the Wayne Williams Atlanta multiple murder case in the early 1980's. Detectives could manipulate information received from informants and tips. It compared information and evidence and gave detectives the current timeline of the crime. They hoped this would help cut through useless information and speed apprehension of a suspect.

Lead #206 came in as a tip from Officer Don Garanson, who worked police detail at the Des Moines International Airport. It was received on December 2nd at nine-fifteen and was assigned to Detectives Westover and Schultz. They met with Garanson who told them that he was called to Avis Car Rental at the airport. An employee there told him that a black male rented a car on November 25th and did not return the car on November 27th as promised. The man identified himself as Darrell Petrie, who listed as his address 2902 Brattleboro in Des Moines. Petrie used a credit card to charge the car. The card was maxed out and the company would not accept the charge. Officer Garanson had initiated a police case as failure to return a leased motor vehicle. Westover and Schultz decided to drive to the listed address and check it out. Parking at the corner of 29th and Brattleboro, they spotted the blue Chevy Lumina with license plate number MSU 132, the leased vehicle that had not been returned.

Detective Westover called Avis Car Rental on his cell phone and told them they had located the vehicle. Avis said they would bring an extra set of keys out immediately and retrieve the car. With the tremendous case load on the detectives, Westover called dispatch and requested that a black-and-white be dispatched to relieve them so they could move on to their next diner case lead. While they were waiting to be relieved, a black Toyota with dark windows passed the officers slowly and pulled into the driveway behind the rental vehicle. A large black man emerged from the car, walked up to the rental car, opened the door and looked inside.

Westover decided it was time to take a look. They pulled up in the street and blocked the driveway. The detectives bailed out, identified themselves and asked the man for his identification. He was Reginald Petrie, Darrell's father, who lived at the residence. He said that Darrell had rented the car, took his mother to New Orleans and had since returned. He did not know why Darrell had not returned the car. Reginald invited the detectives into his home and showed them recent photos of Darrell who was 6' 1" and weighed 225 pounds. After a short discussion, Westover and Shultz glanced at each other, thanked Mr. Petrie for his cooperation, went to their car, called in and closed out the lead as unsubstantiated.

Chapter Three

PRESSURE TO SOLVE the diner murders was coming from all directions. Police Chief Bill Moulder was hearing from everyone: calls came in from local concerned citizens, personal friends in the media, Iowa's congressional representatives in Washington. Moulder's quiet but strong leadership of the Des Moines Police Department served him well during the Drake Diner episode. Appointed chief on September 4th, 1984, he was the only chief appointed from outside the ranks of the Des Moines Police Department. He left the Kansas City Police Department at the rank of major to assume the top position in Des Moines. He was selected from a group of highly qualified candidates for the top job. In Kansas City, he worked in several divisions including assignment as a police helicopter pilot. He underwent pilot training with the Hughes Helicopter Company in San Diego following a demonstration ride with Hughes in Kansas City in 1965.

Moulder loved police work and brought his love of it with him to Des Moines. During his 18-year tenure as chief, he received numerous awards and distinctions for his leadership. His personal manner was controlled and subdued. He insisted on continuous updates on the progress being made in the case. He was also interested in his subordinates' theories and ideas during the investigation. Moulder was leaving communication with the media primarily up to Assistant Chief McCarthy and Lt. Jobe. He emphasized to the entire department repeatedly that he wanted official communications with the media and the public to come through these chosen individuals.

Lieutenant Clarence "Laddie" Jobe was a good choice to speak with the media. "Lad" had a piercing stare and an air of force and firmness. He thought before he spoke during press conferences and didn't say as much as they wanted to hear. He was a complex individual with a zest for challenging and creative work in law enforcement. Jobe was not running a popularity contest with the detectives in his unit. It was comprised of many veteran homicide investigators. He was in charge and there were disagreements but the important thing for a unit of this type was results.

POLICE PERSONNEL reported to Lt. Jobe that they had received a call from Anita Jones, 1517 Washington, who said when she returned home from drug rehab, she discovered that someone had fired a gun in her house while she was away. It left a large, ugly hole in her kitchen floor. Police knew that 1517 Washington was a hangout of the Vice Lords street gang and a drug house. Jobe decided to obtain a search warrant for the house to find the bullet and any other evidence they could that might relate to their investigation. Because of the pressure on the case, the warrant was quickly issued. Jobe and other officers went to the house with the warrant in hand. They found the hole left by the gunshot, traced it into the basement and recovered bullet evidence from the ductwork downstairs. The rest of the detectives investigating the Drake Diner murders, including Rowley, were NOT told about the search warrant or the bullet evidence recovered. However, this was not all that unusual for Jobe.

The name "Cisco" surfaced in the investigation as a suspect through informants and anonymous tips on Monday and Tuesday following the shootings. Police did not have a traceable name to connect to "Cisco." Informants said that he was from Kansas City and traveled back and forth. He fit the physical description that police and the media were circulating. He carried a large black automatic pistol and had a violent temper. Kansas City police said that they had run-ins with "Cisco" in the past. They identified him as Joseph Jerome Gray, Jr., DOB 11/13/70 and described him as "potentially dangerous and probably armed." A female acquaintance in Des Moines, questioned by police, said that he had taken her to the Drake Diner in late October, before the killings. She was reluctant to provide police with other information regarding him – either she didn't know much or she was withholding information. After interviewing her twice, police weren't sure which it was. Further investigation revealed that an anonymous tipster called police on December 2nd saying that, in the week preceding the diner murders, "Cisco" and another black man were seen wearing "big stuffed coats" and acting "suspiciously" at the convenience store at 22nd and University, three blocks from the Drake Diner. The tall, black man with Cisco was driving an older silver four door Chevrolet with Kansas license plates. No license number was reported. While following up on the Cisco lead, Sgt. Ben Klobnak of the Kansas City, Missouri Police called and told Detective Ralph Roth that KCPD had just arrested a convenience store robber who told police that he knew who robbed the Drake Diner and killed those people. After conferring with supervisors, Roth told Sgt. Klobnak to have their detectives find out what this person knew or didn't know and they would follow up – Des Moines investigators were swamped and couldn't spare even one detective for a same day trip to Kansas City.

ONCE DESCRIBED in his yearly evaluation as "the finest homicide detective in the State of Iowa," Jim Rowley had certainly earned the praise and respect of fellow officers and the citizens of Des Moines. A Des Moines Police Officer since 1968, he spent 25 years in the Crimes Against Persons section of the Criminal Investigation Division. The variety of crimes he was assigned to included homicides, robberies, rapes, shootings, harassment cases and many more, he averaged 60 to 90 cases a month.

The clearance rate on his cases was extremely high, even by the high standards of the FBI. Rowley investigated 23 bank robberies, nearly all solved. He worked or was assigned to assist with his expertise on more than 200 homicides, solving 86%. The homicide unit actually solved 38 homicides in a row. Jim Rowley helped to successfully solve the first DNA evidence case in the State of Iowa.

Speaking to a rookie class at the Des Moines Police Academy, Detective Jim Rowley said, "The investigation of homicide is a job that demands anyone who does it has to develop an understanding of the dynamics and principles of proceeding in a professional manner. In the pursuit of justice and the truth, you should gain both knowledge and experience, along with flexibility and common sense."

"At first, even though I'd worked patrol for a long time, I was observing people that were senior to me, many both in age and experience. My idea was that if I was going to work with people in the Crimes Against Persons Section, I had better learn the process. I observed who the sharpest detectives were and I spent time around them. I paid attention and wrote things down. I didn't even realize what impact this would eventually have."

"In the police department, there were basic guidelines for how to use forms and make notifications, but not how to actually solve crimes. The procedure for solving violent crimes in the old days was to pay or pressure informants to give up some leads. There is more to this than getting confessions and rounding up the usual suspects."

"I figured that keeping diaries about my experience reinforced it. I used to keep a list of the experts that I had met in different locations. I would call them up for advice and counsel, ask them this and that, and involve them in the case."

"Five primary components are teamwork, documentation, preservation of evidence, flexibility, and common sense. At a crime scene, investigators are to observe, describe, record whatever they find, and collect any evidence using the proper procedures. In the process, they develop a mental image of the crime. And they must keep in mind that they are all on the same side: they work as a team and share information and strategies. That attitude, I found, was resisted at times, but I kept with it, since there's no such thing as a private investigation. Cops have to work cooperatively."

SEASONED INVESTIGATOR Lt. Jim Trotter had been involved in some of the most complex cases the Des Moines Police Department had ever solved. Certainly, one of the most usual was the Helm case:

William Helm showed up at his mother's place a little before 11:00 a.m. He needed to go to his estranged wife's house to get some tools that he had left there, and he wanted his brother to come with him. He and his wife had a volatile history, and his lawyer advised him against seeing her without another person being present. William arrived at Susan's at about 11:45 p.m. He knocked on the door and there was no answer. William went around to the side of the house and beat on the window. He could see his 15 month-old son, Chucky, in his crib, but neither Susan nor his 4-year-old son, Derrick, were in sight. He went back to the front door, which Derrick finally opened. William picked up the baby from his bed and, followed by his brother, checked the other bedroom.

Susan was lying on her back in bed, partially covered by a blanket. She wasn't moving. William checked her right wrist for a pulse. There was none. His brother called the police from the phone in the kitchen. Officers arrived within minutes and took control of the scene. Over the next 12 hours, Ident technicians gathered forensic evidence from the house, including hair and fiber samples. And from the skin of Susan's upper abdomen, they took something else - a handprint.

"Superglue" was invented by accident in the late 1950's in the labs of Eastman Kodak. The official name for it is "Cyanoacrylate ester adhesive." Cyanoacrylate ester has unique abilities besides bonding surfaces in seconds. A factory worker packaging the product one day happened to notice that when heated in an airtight container, its vapors bond to the faint oily residue left behind by a finger contacting with a surface. As the vapor hardens and builds upon that residue, it becomes visible as a fingerprint. Such residue can be left on many types of surfaces including metal, wood, plastic – and human skin. Lt. Jim Trotter was aware of a new forensic test that put this phenomenon to work in crime solving.

Ident technicians Lee Shaklee and Nancy LeMasters had completed the standard gathering of evidence from the crime scene at Susan Helm's home. Trotter thought they might be missing something. He decided to attempt the "cyanoacrylate fuming" process on the body. The technique was new and nobody had been successful in prosecuting a murder case based on this kind of evidence, but Jim Trotter thought it was worth a shot. From the appearance of the body, it appeared that she had either been strangled or stabbed. It was very likely that the killer had touched her.

Using plastic pipe and a clear plastic drop cloth, they constructed a tent over the body and sealed it with duct tape. They poured superglue into two aluminum dishes, placed each one on a hot plate inside the tent, and turned them on. After 30 minutes they checked the body and found that they didn't have a high enough concentration of fumes to do the job. So they turned up the temperature and tried again.

This time it worked. On Susan Helm's abdomen, just below her right breast, they could see the print of someone's right palm and attempted to lift it from the body. It didn't work but the photos were very clear. The print itself would not be necessary. The primary suspect from the beginning was Susan's husband, William Helm. Detective Rahn Bjornson obtained a search warrant that enabled him to collect William Helm's fingerprints.

When a latent print (one that is taken from the scene of a crime), is compared to the known print of a suspect, the technician is looking for points of comparison: tiny curls, breaks and ridges in the lines of a fingerprint that are exactly the same in the latent, and the suspect's prints. When technicians Robert Baker and Jerry Wilson compared William Helm's prints with the photo of the print on Susan Helm's body, they needed eight points of comparison to prove that the latent belonged to Helm. They stopped counting at 96.

Jim Trotter presented his evidence to the court in his professional manner and the jury agreed with his discoveries. William Helm was sentenced to life in prison without parole for the killing of his wife Susan. The case remains the only one in history where a murderer was convicted by a palm print found on a body itself using the cyanoacrylate fuming process. [5]

TUESDAY EVENING, December 1st, Rowley, Singleton and several others were called to the station to meet with Lt. Jobe and police intelligence. Intelligence had developed a suspect named Kevin Jenkins who was on intensive parole supervision. His name had popped up immediately following the Drake Diner homicides and the intelligence unit had followed the lead on their own as they often did. Their mission allowed them to follow unconventional avenues as they saw fit. In the Drake Diner case, they saw this as assisting with the tremendous case overload in their own fashion. Along with members of the tactical unit, they executed a search warrant at Jenkins' residence at 713 College. Jenkins was not located but people there said that he was staying with his girlfriend at 5201 South Union, apartment 205. Police then obtained a second search warrant for that location. Occupants who were at 713 College were kept from phoning or otherwise warning anyone of police intentions.

At 3:45 a.m., officers executed the South Union search warrant. The only persons there were Tanya Wickler and her two young children, one a newborn. Rowley and Singleton questioned her. She was, indeed, Kevin Jenkins' girlfriend and the two children were theirs together. Asked where they could find Kevin, she said that Kevin's mother had called and said his name was on the police radio and that he was wanted for questioning in the murders. She said he panicked and left the apartment in her car. Asked about Sunday night, she said that they had been together and had four witnesses to prove it who lived right there in the building. Officers put out a stop and hold on Tanya Wickler's '86 Plymouth.

ON WEDNESDAY, DECEMBER 2nd, the third day after the killings, people opening up *The Des Moines Register* read the headline "Police find killings difficult to solve." Pressure was mounting daily on every front for a break in the case. Assistant Chief Bill McCarthy was quoted in The Register as having said he 'thought the killer is local.' He said that the crime was solvable but right now it is slim going. He thought they were in for the grind right now. The Register followed McCarthy's published statement with an article titled "Experts say they don't think the killer is from Des Moines." The experts quoted were Ray Cornell, a local private investigator, and Dean Wright, a Drake University sociologist.[6]

The media continued by quizzing McCarthy concerning the "expert interviews." McCarthy said that he would not comment on news reports or speculation suggesting possible suspects and motives in the Drake Diner murders. Additionally he said that no information had been authorized by his division or the department. For all of the media's sanctimony about their commitment to the facts, racial polarizing and theorizing about who the murderer might be quickly began.

Jobe conducted the press briefings. It could be a tough job but he was the right person for it. He had to act and speak forcefully and convincingly without divulging investigation details or making any promises. As time wore on, some reporters were beginning to smart off to him, not feeling they were getting the whole story. "We'll have a vote and if it's decided that the media should be the organization that's going to solve this case, then, the case is yours," Jobe said sarcastically during the Wednesday morning press conference. Police had several eyewitnesses and informants who were working with police investigators but officially the Des Moines Police Department had announced no suspect in the shootings.

In further comments to reporters, Jobe said leaks could compromise the investigation. He said the media should *not* be the ones trying to solve this case." I hope that everyone will have the same attitude. They should not be the 'conduit' of bad, incorrect or misleading information that could harm the case's progress," Jobe said. He said that the media, by reporting to people in the community about possible profiles and motives of the killer, could lead to people having "closed minds" about who the real suspect might be. Jobe also criticized what he called the "talking heads," which was an apparent reference to some police officers, former police officials and others acting as media consultants.

He suggested that such consultants might have been "unsuccessful" during their police careers and just wanted to promote themselves. He urged them to stop giving interviews and "theorizing." "We've got officials and others claiming to be 'in-the-know' out there looking to get their faces on TV," Jobe said. "If they are naming names and making reference to the progress of the ongoing investigation so they can have the pleasure of being seen on TV news, we just don't need it! I know what they are trying to do, but I also plead with them to stop this conduct now. Let our police officers do their job." He added that if someone suspected another person or thought they might know something to please contact police. They did not mind chasing what might turn out to be empty leads in this case.

At 9:15 a.m., Kevin Jenkins unexpectedly walked in to the detective office downtown accompanied by his attorney Ben Walker. Jobe called Rowley and Singleton in and they interviewed Jenkins behind closed doors, taping the interview. Ninety minutes later, Jenkins and his lawyer left police headquarters. The normally taciturn Lt. Jobe asked Rowley what happened. Jim Rowley said in a disappointed tone, "It's not him. His alibis in his building have no reason to be covering for him. We've added him to a photo spread anyway…it's just not him." Rowley turned and walked away without further comment.

The Drake Bulldogs Basketball Team had a practice set for 5:00 a.m., Wednesday, December 3rd, at the Knapp Center. Six detectives walked into that early practice. Jim Rowley announced, "We are here about the Drake Diner killings. Some of you were present at the diner before, during and after the murders of those two innocent individuals and we want any information that you might have with regard to what happened that night. Some of you saw the killer. Some of you can help us to find the killer. You all go to Drake. Whether you are from here or not, this is a matter of civic responsibility in my mind – two people died for no reason. These victims were white and the killer is black. It could have just as easily been the other way around. We are here to solve a vicious, vicious crime." Following that, detectives moved the interviewee/witnesses up into the stands and conducted one-on-one interviews. Coach Rudy Washington stood down on the playing floor with his arms crossed, glaring angrily at the interviewing detectives.

Detectives first interviewed Ray Slater, a junior at Drake and a varsity basketball player. He said that he had just finished eating that night and as he was leaving the diner, he bumped into an individual wearing a gray, full-face ski mask. The mask was pulled down. He stated that this person was holding the gun upright, not hidden. His description of the weapon was a black automatic, possibly a 9-millimeter, with some sort of red light on it. His description of the assailant was a light complexioned black man, skinny, 5' 8" to 5' 11", clean-shaven. Slater observed him pull up the mask as he approached the hostess' stand. He did see the assailant go around and shoot the female victim in the head. Asked if he could identify the assailant, he paused momentarily and then said he could not.

It was reported to officers that the coach's son, Drake player Rudy Washington, Jr. exchanged words with the gunman in the entrance of the diner. According to witnesses, the shooter said Washington "was lucky he was black or he'd be dead." Interviews were also conducted with Kevin Patrick Murphy, manager of the basketball team, who was with Ray Slater. His statement was much the same as Ray Slater's. Assistant Coach of the Drake Bulldogs, Patrick Rafferty, gave a fairly detailed description of the shooter although he couldn't venture an accurate guess as to his age. Drake team members Adrian Thomas and Curt Smith provided descriptions that coincided with the others. Results of the Drake interviews were added to the case file that was growing by the hour. Investigators had hoped that the Drake team could offer more help than they ended up providing.

RIGHT AFTER the murders, signs had gone up near the doors of the Diner saying that they were closed. Wreaths, flowers and crosses surrounded the front of the building. The weather seemed unusually cold and damp. The owner and the management team at the Drake Diner were determined from the time of this tragedy to pay homage to their fallen friends and their families, and to reopen the diner as quickly as possible. A professional cleaning company had been contracted to come in and restore the interior of the building. Blood and body fluids had seeped into areas that were tough to clean up. The cleaning company told the diner owners that unless the job was done right, remains could return as a thin pink powder that has an odd odor. It was a major undertaking on a tight schedule.

Bill Knapp's spokesman, Doug Shaffer, announced that the diner would reopen at 7:00 a.m. Friday morning, December 4th.

He said that the day's proceeds would be donated to establish funds for the families of the victims. He also said that all of the diner employees were returning. Doug Shaffer spoke on behalf of Mr. Knapp at a candle light vigil honoring the two victims, attended by more than 150 people and held in the blustery weather on Tuesday night. Many of Tim and Cara's coworkers were in attendance. People were unwilling to let the tragedy ruin all of the hard work that had gone into revitalizing the Drake neighborhood and establishments like the Drake Diner that enjoyed great, new business there. They pledged to stand steadfast against the fear and anxiety this had caused.

Tim Burnett's funeral was held at 2:00 p.m. on Wednesday, December 2nd at Merle Hay Funeral Home. The funeral home was jammed with people. The visitation the night before found every room full of mourners and a line waiting in the cold outside the funeral home. It was open casket, according to Drake Diner owner Steve Vilmain. It demonstrated the unusual talent of the morticians in preserving the handsome appearance of Tim Burnett before this tragic event. Most attendees assumed earlier it would be closed casket under the circumstances.

The officiating pastor at the funeral told mourners "Tim was light." He talked about Tim's life and read from the same Bible passage that was part of Tim and Mary's wedding – Saint Paul's beautiful essay on "Love" from the thirteenth chapter of First Corinthians, "Love is patient. Love is kind . . . Love does not come to an end." People who knew Tim cried openly during the ceremony. It was a sharp, blustery afternoon outside and mourners huddled together and shivered at the burial site on the slope of a snowy hill. People who knew him still could not believe he was gone. They said it was such a senseless tragedy.

The media blitz to solve the shootings was unrelenting. The mood was reflected in published statements: "A dark sadistic killer seems to stay one step ahead of the police." Reporters were relentless with the Des Moines Police Department coaxing every lead that they could find. Politicians, civic leaders, community activists and media representatives wanted to know *when* this crime was going to be solved. Responding to a barrage of questions, police spokesman Sgt. Ray Rexroat said, "We will do whatever it takes. If it takes ten years – we're not willing to put a timeline on this." People said, "Ten years? Ten days is too long!" Official press briefings were continuing twice each day. The Des Moines Downtown Auto Dealers added $20,000 to the reward, doubling the amount offered. Another development of significance was that the murder weapon was now identified as a "Grizzly" as opposed to a Desert Eagle. Firearms experts had raised that possibility of it being a Grizzly early on. Investigators thought this was an important detail to keep to themselves until a suspect was in custody and could be questioned, but pressure on this case demanded that any clue that would help solve this case had to be made public.

The Grizzly Win Mag pistols were designed and invented in the 1980's by Peter Arnett. He patented the technology under U.S. Patent # 4,253,377 licensed to L.A.R. Manufacturing Inc. Following their introduction to shooters, it was believed to be the most powerful handgun in the world. The pistols were essentially an up-scale Colt M 1911. Many parts were interchangeable. But instead of the standard .45 ACP fired by the M 1911, later models could fire the .44 Magnum, the .50 ACP or the .50 AE. Because of the large size, weight and hefty recoil of the weapon, the primary market for sales was hunting and for protection of sportsmen who hunt in areas where big game could be a threat. The loads were adequate for North American big game within range, including the great bears. It would provide protection to a sportsman surprised by a bear who was forced to shoot in brush or heavy timber.

Identifying the murder weapon as an L.A.R. Grizzly Mark IV .44 Magnum became a focal point in the Drake Diner case. The Des Moines Police Department requested the assistance of the U.S. Department of the Treasury, Division of Alcohol, Tobacco, and Firearms (ATF) to determine the number of Grizzlys in .44 Magnum caliber that were distributed to firearms merchants by the gun's manufacturer. Police thought that the Grizzly was a rare firearm. They couldn't remember a case involving one. Following interviews with L.A.R., ATF reported to the Des Moines Police Intelligence Unit that only 450 .44 Magnum Grizzlys had been shipped to gun dealers. ATF delivered the complete list of recipients. Grizzlys had been shipped all over the country, including several to the State of Alaska.

L.A.R. .44 Magnum Grizzly Semi-Automatic Handgun

The task now was to determine exactly where the 450 Grizzlys were currently located. Assignments were made to Des Moines investigating detectives covering roughly three states each using the ATF lists (based on the number of guns shipped to that area.) They were to contact the dealers who took delivery of the Grizzlys and establish who purchased these guns - then find the owners and verify the current location of the gun. The number of guns sent to each particular state prioritized the lists. Some states had many more than others. Detective Singleton drew the two states of Michigan and New Jersey; Ralph Roth was assigned the states of Kentucky, Louisiana and Maryland; Jim Rowley drew the State of Alaska; and Bill Boggs had the State of Washington.

Most detectives looked at this as a long shot at best. They immediately saw that they were going to have to enlist the assistance of local law enforcement in their assigned states to verify whereabouts of these weapons. Phone calls were made to the police jurisdictions where the guns had been shipped. Local officers in those jurisdictions were assigned responsibility for making contact with the individual gun shops. The lists involved a lot of work and phone calls to verify and complete. Officers felt the work would become tedious, unproductive and time consuming – it was. In an unrelated and unproductive search for evidence, officers under the supervision of Sgt. Jerry Jones searched through 2500 pounds of trash and garbage at the solid waste transfer facility that came from the immediate area of the diner after the shooting. They used hoes and pitchforks in what Assistant Chief Nick Brown characterized to the press as "a long shot."

Efforts by five specially trained officers from other law enforcement agencies failed to draw up a satisfactory psychological profile of the Drake Diner killer. They had so little to work with. The details of the single crime and the description of the killer contained no clues to patterns of any kind. In addition, many of the detectives assigned to the case had been working 12 to 16 hour shifts since the case opened. They were showing signs of short-term burn out and fatigue, indicating that, if they continued, they could not be depended on to do the precise investigative work that they were known for. Officers from West Des Moines and the Polk County Sheriff's Office were also assigned to assist in the investigation. Des Moines investigators began asking for time off and based on the pressure of the case – supervisors denied it. Signs of stress and frustration were becoming more commonplace.

Bill Smith got home from a 13-hour day of Drake Diner follow-up and was faced by his wife, Audrey, in an obviously hostile mood. She asked him who the woman was that had called their house twice looking for him. Not in the mood, Bill asked her the name of the woman. His wife answered, "just Michelle!" Bill was too tired to argue about it. He shook his head and said it was a woman who says she might have information on the diner case and he left it at that. She yelled, "Why is she calling here? Why is she calling you? I am so sick of this. We haven't seen you since this happened! Are you going out on me?" She threw his bed pillow out onto the couch in the family room and stomped off to bed. Bill got a beer and made a nest on the couch for the night. He returned to work at 6:00 a.m. the following morning and gathered his new leads.

Police had another new lead. Several calls came in to police on a man named Kenneth Wilson. He was black, in the right range of height and callers said he was "crazy." Detectives began pulling records and assembling a picture of Kenneth G. Wilson. People familiar with Wilson included police officers, attorneys and neighbors. Local attorney Bill Thomas related that he was advising Wilson once on a legal matter when Wilson physically attacked him for no apparent reason. Officers soon discovered Wilson was a walk away from the Sands Mental Health Unit at Broadlawns Hospital in Des Moines. There was also a warrant for his arrest for parole violation. Interviewed neighbors told the officers that Wilson had been seen with a large handgun, had made threats, wore a three quarter length black and gray Los Angeles Kings coat similar to the description of the killer's dress and, most important – he'd been seen wearing bloody clothing following the murders at the diner. Assistant Chief McCarthy told investigators to "find Kenneth Wilson now!" Police set up an around the clock stake out of his residence. Trotter and Rowley told Chief McCarthy that the report of Kenneth Wilson wearing bloody clothing probably wasn't of much significance with regard to the murder scene that night. The diner suspect wasn't visibly bloodied when he exited the scene of the crime. McCarthy said, "Find him."

Jobe, Ervin, Roth and Rowley were called into a meeting in Chief Bill Moulder's first floor office at headquarters early

Thursday morning. When everyone was finally in the room, Chief Moulder closed the door. Moulder, Chief of Detectives Bill McCarthy, Polk County Sheriff Bob Rice, Polk County Attorney John Sarcone and assistant Polk County attorney Steve Foritano were there - looking to the detectives for new developments. Following several statements about local politicians talking to the media, Moulder looked over at the detectives and said, "The pressure on this case is getting worse. Everybody's on the bandwagon for whatever political mileage they can get. We are really under the gun for results – positive results – now! I'm looking at reports from our crews on this and the reports aren't telling me anything substantial. The news media are chewing us up here! Find the SOB that did this!" Jobe said they had some solid leads they were working on and people were coming around and talking to detectives. He added that these cases take time if they aren't solved quickly. Moulder glared at Jobe and looked back at his detectives and said, "Give me something!"

McCarthy and Rowley walked out of the chief's office together. McCarthy turned to him outside and said, "It's getting bad. What they are referring to is that Mike McPherson, our city councilman, has requested access from the mayor and city manager to all of our investigative files on this case. He told them that he wants to try to determine if we are doing everything possible to solve this case - McPherson determining if we were doing everything!" Rowley said from experience - McPherson's real reason was all about politics, as usual - to feed his media cronies information that made him the "man in the know" and, unfortunately, he had the potential to compromise the case to satisfy his own personal agenda. McCarthy said the mayor and city manager had criticized him for having so many police personnel *milling around at the crime scene on city time*, as they called it. McCarthy snapped back at them and told them that the confluence of law enforcement professionals was absolutely necessary: they had detectives; ident; crowd control;

senior commanders; witness interviews and evidence gathering to do and that takes people. The whole situation was becoming increasingly frustrating for everyone.

Sgt. Larry Pendarvis, DMPD Internal Affairs, stopped Laddie Jobe in the hall and asked him to stop by his office. Jobe came into his office, told him he was real busy and closed the door. Pendarvis told him that an old neighborhood informant of his, Lucretia Wright, who lived on 23rd Street, called him and said that Nick Young, usually a dependable snitch, told her that "Turk", a/k/a Tommy Joe Johnson was apparently broke prior to Sunday, the day of the killings. But on Monday, he reportedly was packing a handgun at a party on Mondamin, laughed and joked about the Drake Diner murders, said they got what they deserved and had a lot of cash to gamble on dice and cards. Jobe scanned Turk's rap sheet that Pendarvis gave him, handed it back and asked him to call upstairs and get a lead sheet made out for it. Jobe said he was just too busy to deal with it at that moment. All of the detectives, including supervisors, were beginning to feel overwhelmed by the volume of information that was coming in that needed attention on this case.

Chapter Four

EIGHT HUNDRED people attended Cara McGrane's funeral on Thursday, December 3rd at Holy Trinity Catholic Church near her home in the Beaverdale area of northwest Des Moines. Father James Laurenzo officiated at the ceremony basing his eulogy and message on the Saint Francis prayer. Laurenzo said, "We can ask why, but there are never reasonable answers to senseless acts. Cara's death should serve as a call to action against handguns." [7] Father Laurenzo later said that the McGrane family had requested a message of gun control be incorporated into the eulogy. He said later that it was an extremely hard funeral mass to perform under the circumstances. The media carried extensive coverage of the funeral. The expressed and open sadness of those who knew this wonderful, energetic young woman was heart-wrenching.

The same day, right after lunch, Rowley and Singleton met with a longtime police informant named Carmen with whom Rowley had worked. Carmen was a flashy, light skinned black woman in her forties. Her brother had been murdered five years earlier and Jim Rowley had arrested his killer. For that, Carmen was grateful and Jim considered her a friend. She heard a lot of people talk around town. Carmen told them that she had a "friend" who apparently had information concerning the murders at the diner. The "friend" wanted to remain anonymous - at least for the present time. The following information was given to Carmen, who in turn contacted Jim:

The new informant told Carmen that the shooter was "Freddy Clark." Carmen asked her if this was Alf Freddy Clark - she said it was. Alf Freddy Clark was a seventeen-year-old black juvenile who was associated with the Vice Lords street gang. The new informant said that Clark lived someplace south of Forest Avenue off of 21st Street with his mother and he was running with a cousin by the name of "Joe." The informant wasn't sure of the exact address. Directions given were to go to 21st Street and Forest, then turn left, go two more blocks and turn right. Detectives concluded that would be near the 2200 block of Carpenter if this were correct. She said Joe was believed to be from Texas and was supposedly wanted there for murder. The informant further stated that in the Anita Jones residence at 1517 Washington Avenue, a .44 Magnum handgun had been fired. The .44 round went through a counter and into the basement.

Carmen said that according to this woman, after the robbery and murders, the shooter, Freddy Clark, ran to a nearby house somewhere on 24th Street, staying there where he would be able to watch all of the activity following the shooting. Clark had admitted to the informant that he was the shooter. The .44 Magnum was reportedly brought to Des Moines from Chicago in a shipment of guns sent to the Vice Lords. In Chicago, there was a turf war between the Vice Lords and the BGDs (Black Gangster Disciples) and they decided to move their cache of weapons out of town. She said that later on the night of the Drake Diner murders, Freddy Clark and his cousin Joe went to the 1517 Washington address and Clark's cousin Joe fired a round from the .44 that ended up in the basement. The informant emphasized that what she said had to be kept secret and confidential because they would know who the source was. Only four individuals knew the identity of the shooter. The new informant said that she would be killed if word got out.

She went on with more information: There had been a large amount of money taken in the Drake Diner robbery and the killers were spending it like crazy. On the First of December, they rented the Presidential Suite at the Downtown Holiday Inn for approximately $167 and had a party. A woman named Barb Hagen or Hogan reserved the room. The informant let it be known that she was not interested in the substantial reward, with the exception of one thing: she hoped to receive two-thousand dollars so they could pay off the mortgage on her mother's house. She told Carmen that officers of the Des Moines Police Department had already questioned her and she was not interested in cooperating with those particular officers because she feared for her life.

After the detectives initially met with Carmen, they returned to police headquarters and shared this new information with Lt. Jobe and Sgt. Ervin. With Laddie Jobe and Jim Rowley, a sense of competition always hovered in the background of their relationship. Jobe insisted that they make the informant available to them for further questioning. Rowley refused and said that the informant had already dealt with other Des Moines Police officers that she had no trust in and she was in fear for her life. Jobe pressed the point and tempers flared. Rowley threatened to go to Chief Moulder and County Attorney John Sarcone to protect his witness. Jobe backed off. Jobe said that the surveillance teams on suspect Kenneth Wilson's place hadn't located him yet and they were looking at Wilson with major interest. Jobe asked Rowley what he knew about Kenneth Wilson's involvement or the hunt for him. Rowley said nothing and walked out.

Rowley and Singleton left the station and paid a visit to the Holiday Inn Downtown. They walked in the lobby, went to the desk and asked to speak with the manager. A man in a Holiday Inn blazer approached them and said, "I'm Gene Caleb, the General Manager. How can I help you?"

Rowley showed him his badge and ID and said, "We need some information. We were told that a group of individuals rented your Presidential Suite on the night of December First.

Is that true?" Caleb said that it was true, then went and retrieved his record of the stay.

"Yes," he said. "A Barb Hogan of 1042 18th Street checked in with a party of four sometime after eleven that night and they checked out shortly after noon the next day. Our employee Shirley Duffy was on the night desk."

Rick Singleton asked him if, by any chance, they had made any phone calls. Manager Caleb looked at the card and said, "They made two calls. One was at 1:35 a.m. to Paul Revere's Pizza at 277-6151. The second call was to a phone at 288-4636 at 2:35 a.m.." The detectives asked for and received two copies of the hotel receipts showing Barb Hogan as the hotel guest. They thanked Mr. Caleb, went to the car and started back for the station.

Rick Singleton looked over at Rowley in the car and said, "When our Mr. Caleb confirmed the information, I got a little chill. Now, I'm fired up." Jim Rowley said they would go put the receipts in property and then they would follow the trail of this just as far as it took them.

At the station, Singleton put in a call to the home of Shirley Duffy, the night desk attendant at the hotel.

"Shirley Duffy?"

"Yes."

"This is Detective Richard Singleton, Des Moines Police Department. We just spoke with Mr. Gene Caleb, manager of the hotel. He said that you were working the night desk at the hotel on December first. Is that true?"

"Yes."

"Do you remember a group of people who rented the Presidential Suite that night?"

"Yes, I do."

"What do you remember about that?"

"Well, a woman came in and checked in and then went back out and a group of four people walked through the lobby in a hurry and went up to the Presidential Suite. One of the men had a sack that I assume was full of booze. Two more people came in later and joined them. I thought it was a little strange because the man with Barb looked very young."

"What did he look like?"

"He was a black guy, tall, thin. Six foot, maybe 160 pounds. He wore a long coat and a beret and he was carrying the sack. There was another guy."

"What did he look like?"

"Oh, black, 5'8" maybe 140 pounds. He looked young, too - short hair and a brown leather coat. The other two people were black women."

"What about the two visitors later?"

"I'm not real sure about them."

"The others - could you identify them if you saw them again?"

"Oh, yes."

Singleton thanked her, hung up and documented the call on a supplemental report. He turned to Jim Rowley and said, "I wonder what else this informant knows?"

Rowley and Singleton thought they might be on the right track on the new information they had received. They passed it on and discussed it in the morning briefing. After the briefing, Trotter called them in for a meeting in his office with key Ident personnel. Lt. Trotter said, "We have some interesting news: The bullets from the diner murders match the bullets that were recovered from the Isaac Newsome party shooting case. It was the same gun used in both incidents. Newsome was shot through the window of his house during a gang party, shot in the crotch. Okay, McCarthy and Jobe know that much. But there's more," He squinted at them both and said, "You guys know Andre Jenkins, don't you?" They both acknowledged run-ins with him in the past. He continued, "Well I've got news – we got a tip from Cedric Howe, the drug dealer and informant who talks to us to keep his ass out of jail for coke. He says that Andre IS the shooter. He told us that Isaac Newsome slapped Andre's girlfriend at Buschwacker's Bar and Andre found out about it and told people he was going to kill him. Our people out there say Andre is packing a "sizable" piece and I'm not talking about in his pants either. The rounds are a match. I'll pass this on to Jobe and dispatch. Let's put out a stop on him as a material witness."

By Thursday, the police department had 460 leads in the murder investigation. 100 had been cleared so far, but Assistant Chief Nick Brown said at a briefing that, due to the stress on manpower, they had 60 leads that had not been assigned yet. Late that night the stakeout crew on Kenneth Wilson's apartment reported that Wilson had just returned home. Detectives had prepared a search warrant request and word that the stakeout crew now had him under surveillance started the process of obtaining the warrant. Based on the evidence, Judge Anthony Critelli signed a search warrant authorizing a search of Kenneth Wilson: a blood sample from Wilson, a search of his 1981 Toyota Celica two-door and his apartment at 707 Forest Avenue. Items sought were one dark jacket with sports logo, any and all bloody clothes and a handgun and ammunition.

When detectives and tactical officers hit the apartment within the hour, they searched his apartment and placed Kenneth Wilson under arrest for parole violation. They noticed that Wilson's left arm was bandaged and his right elbow was wrapped as well. He also had a stitch on the back of his right hand. They found the coat described with blood stains on it, as well as blue jeans and a t-shirt with bloodstains. No handgun was found. All evidence was confiscated and sent to the DCI lab for analysis. Detectives questioned Wilson on the third floor of police headquarters. Wilson had a court appointed attorney to represent him during questioning. Wilson was belligerent and uncooperative during the interrogation, telling detectives to "figure it out yourselves."

THE DRAKE DINER reopened for business at 7:00 a.m. on Friday, December 4th. The outside temperature was fifteen degrees. There was a line outside from 7:00 a.m. until closing that night. Four hundred Drake area residents carrying banners marched to the diner in support of the Drake community. They handed out flyers stating, "We love our neighborhood and unity will prevail." The message from the "Diner family" was "We vow to carry on." City Councilman Preston Daniels told the crowd, "Crime is not going to drive us away from our neighborhood." Bill Plymat, Jr., president of the Drake Neighborhood Association, continued, "We're here tonight to say together to the entire city that we're going to keep doing the things that we've been doing over the years. We've worked hard to make this a good, safe neighborhood for all kinds of people." Bill Knapp added, "It's hard for me to accept the deaths of Cara and Tim. But it would also be tough for me if all the work that has been done here has been in vain." The message on the diner's chalkboard said "God Bless the Diner Family." [8] Local officials including Police Chief Bill Moulder, several police officers, City Council members, firefighters, Drake University professors and media representatives were among the people in the line who patiently waited to enter the diner. Donations that day exceeded $20,000. Donations to the reward came from Younkers, the Drake Neighborhood Association, Boswell's Restaurant and Hawkeye Bank among others. The Iowa Restaurant and Beverage Association contributed $10,000. The total donations to the reward fund now stood at $68,350.

Most officers on the Des Moines Police Department would agree that the two most knowledgeable experts on firearms were Capt. Kayne Robinson, decorated Vietnam veteran, and veteran detective Warren Martin. Certainly, there were many others who knew guns considering the nature of this profession, but these two individuals were standouts. Martin could teardown, service and re-assemble any firearm. He could identify nearly any gun from blurry surveillance camera footage following convenience store holdups. He amazed young officers with his collective knowledge of weaponry. In either a demonstration or competition he had fired nearly every weapon that anyone could describe. On Tuesday following the diner killings, he demonstrated for a press gathering the power of a .44 Magnum by firing a .44 Magnum Desert Eagle into a milk jug filled with water. The jug exploded instantly showering everyone with water. Warren Martin's interest in guns made the Drake Diner case irresistible. Martin came into work on Friday morning and found a note to call Darwin McCoy. McCoy was a reloader-shooter friend of Martin's who drove over-the-road trucks. His note said that he followed the news and he had a lead on a Grizzly, possibly stolen. Martin wasted no time calling him on McCoy's cell phone. "Darwin, it's Warren Martin, Des Moines Police. I got your message. What have you got?"

Darwin replied, "Hey Warren, I've been hearing all this week about those killings at that Drake Diner in Des Moines. Now they say the murder weapon's a Grizzly .44. I know this guy, a fellow teamster, named Gary Forrester, who brought a Grizzly .44 in a nice wooden case to a gun show in Moline last year. I talked to him a couple of months ago and he said his house had been kicked in while he was on the road and he said they took a whole bunch of his stuff. Of course, this was before this shit went down in Des Moines, but I got to wonderin' if Forrester's gun might have been taken. I tried to call him yesterday and today but he hasn't returned my calls."

Detective Martin asked him, "Where does he live at? His place of record?"

"Monroe, Wisconsin – southern Wisconsin."

"We've got a detective assigned to track down all Grizzlys in Wisconsin. Let me find out who that is and pass this information on for follow-up. Give me your call back number . . ."

ALSO ON FRIDAY, Jim Rowley received a call from their informant, Carmen, with the "friend" who had information. The detectives wanted to set up a meeting with this new female informant. She was not comfortable with that, but was willing to be interviewed by Detective Rowley over the phone as long as it was not recorded on tape. Rick Singleton listened in on another phone silently as the interview began.

She said that she had been riding around with her friends on Sunday night and they ended up at a house. At about 10:30 p.m. "Freddy C" came to the house with his cousin Joe. Joe was carrying a "very big" black gun that looked like the gun she had seen on TV. The two of them were whispering a lot. Most everyone at the house was sitting in the living room. Joe walked into the kitchen and that was when the gun went off. Following that, Joe cut up the carpet where the bullet went in and Freddy C tried to dig the lead out of the floor and then the two left the house. She saw the whole thing, saying that she walked into the kitchen following the shot, and Joe said "anybody who talks about this will get *smoked*." To her knowledge Freddy and Joe were almost always armed.

As the phone conversation continued, she said that Joe was the only one with a gun that particular night. She overheard conversation between Freddy and Joe about the shooting, money and something about a *.44 to the head*. It was very unusual for Freddy C or Joe to have any money at all. But on Tuesday night Freddy C said, "Let's go to a hotel." That night at the hotel Joe had "all sorts of money."

Rowley asked her, "Who went to the hotel?"

She said, "Joe, Freddy C, Barb, me and my friend."

"Barb Hogan was with you at the hotel?"

"Yes."

"Uh-huh. What else can you tell us that might help?"

"Joe got real drunk and was joking about shooting people in the head. He said if anybody snitched on him, he'd have to whack them. Freddy was acting real nervous. It seemed like everything that they talked about was murder. Freddy said that these white people deserved what happened. He's got something against white people. He's depressed, not changing clothes and talking about suicide. These guys were saying that something big was going to happen this Sunday and then they were leaving town."

"Have you actually seen this gun we are talking about?" Rowley asked her.

"Yes, I have. I saw it at Freddy C's crib and at the hotel that night."

"What else?"

"They were planning an alibi. They were gonna say that they were at Tammy's crib at the time it happened, but they weren't really there. They were hanging around during the time the diner investigation was going on. Everybody's saying that Joe is wanted for murder in Texas. He is very nervous around the police. So is Freddy. He was in a car the other night that was stopped by the police and he was petrified."

"Describe Joe to me."

"He's black, 16 or 17, about 5' 8", big feet, dresses in red or black and has a gap in his teeth."

"What about Freddy C? How would you describe him?"

"Black, tall and thin, with a gold tooth and crooked bottom teeth."

"Anything else?"

"No. That's everything I can think of right now."

They concluded the interview and were convinced by the evidence they had, that the informant was being truthful. Jim Rowley thought they had adequate evidence to seek search warrants and take Freddy Clark and his cousin "Joe" into custody. They discussed this with supervisors and everyone agreed that these two individuals needed to be brought in.

WITH THE ACCUMULATION of relevant evidence surrounding the murders, particularly this confidential informant's dead-on accounts of the weapon, the night at the hotel and the suspect, police decided it was time to move and quickly. Chief McCarthy told them to "find the kid with the gap in his teeth and find the gun." Detectives huddled and decided it was time to meet with the Polk County Attorney's Office and begin the process of obtaining search warrants. Warrants were to be executed at 1517 Washington Avenue where the Grizzly was discharged, and 2212 Carpenter Street. These residences were believed to be where these suspects could be located and taken into custody.

Rowley and Singleton talked with DMPD Sgt. Dick Kail about 2212 Carpenter. Kail led a search of that house previously on a separate case. These officers wanted to know what the house was like, the layout inside and what they might expect. Kail said they located a reported runaway juvenile girl at the house on his case. He said it would be hard to accurately predict what they might run into there. When Kail searched the house, there were two black older women downstairs. Upstairs there were six "gang bangers", some wearing Oakland Raider jackets, in one room. In another bedroom there was a blonde, white female in bed with a black male with curls in his hair who Kail thought was Alf Freddy Clark. Kail said the house sat on the south side of Carpenter and was a standard older two story in rather dilapidated condition.

LATE ON THE MORNING of Saturday, the fifth of December, Jim Rowley met at the County Attorney's office with Assistant County Attorneys Ray Blase and James Ramey. Since they believed the suspect to possibly be a juvenile, juvenile officer Burt Aunan was in attendance along with a female clerk recording the proceedings. The process of preparing the search warrants with specifics took nearly five hours.

There was concern voiced over the choice of Polk County judges to approach with the search warrants for signature prior to their execution. The choice was made to contact the toughest one they knew, Judge Anthony Critelli. Judge Critelli was considered the best judge in terms of jurisprudence. His decisions were seldom, if ever, overturned according to Jim Rowley. County Attorney Ramey called Judge Critelli at home.

He and Rowley went to the judge's home in the early afternoon with the search warrants that they had labored over all morning for completeness and accuracy. When they arrived, Judge Critelli answered the door and invited the men into his home. Ramey wasted no time handing the judge the search warrants. Judge Critelli gave both men a slow, serious glance and smiled. He invited the officers into his study and asked them to have a seat. The judge sat down, put on his reading glasses and carefully read the warrants. He stopped from time-to-time to re-read phrasing and details. When he was finished reading the warrants, he rose, looked at Rowley and Ramey over his glasses and said, "Do you mind if I re-read this?" They said that was fine. The judge sat back down and re-read the documents. When he finished the second reading, he stood up, looked at Rowley and said, "Raise your hand, officer, and swear to this as factual in every respect." Jim Rowley swore to the accuracy of the document. The judge concluded by saying, "Good hunting, Officer Rowley. This search warrant will never be overturned." With warrants in hand, Rowley returned to the station to begin the tactical implementation of the process.

The search warrant for the 2212 Carpenter address specified that it was a private residence occupied by Zella Williams and her son Alf Freddy Clark. It went on to say that the persons and property covered by the warrant were Alf Freddy Clark, Jeremy Jerome Spenser, Ray Spenser, and a person known to investigators only as "Joe." In addition, any other persons present at the address, all vehicles present at the address, the house, outbuildings and curtilage and a 1977 silver Chevrolet four-door automobile with an "in-transit" hand lettered sign in the window in lieu of license plates.

The items sought were a .44 caliber semi-automatic handgun, described as dark in color, ammunition for a .44 caliber weapon, a variety of clothing items to include any bloodied clothing, blood stained wash cloths or towels, cash, evidence of blood residue in sinks or basins, any items with blood stains or gunshot residues. The warrant permitted the taking of fingerprints, blood specimens and photographs of Alf Freddy Clark and the person named Joe for use in the investigation of the case. The warrant said that the items were sought because they were: property which was obtained in violation of the law, and/or property that was illegally possessed, and/or property used or possessed with the intent to be used to commit a public offense or concealed to prevent the offense from being discovered, and/or property relevant and material as evidence in a criminal prosecution or investigation. It was signed at 3:35 p.m. on the Fifth of December, 1992, by Judge Critelli.

Selected officers were quietly assembling at police headquarters to be part of the teams that would serve the search warrants in this headline case. Some officers had special stun weapons, some had small video cameras to record what happened and others wore protective assault vests for the initial entry. Everyone was charged up for execution of the warrants.

Several days prior to the murders, Lt. Jobe and Sgt. Bob Ervin decided on a whim to buy new business suits and they went to the New York Exchange Suit Company in downtown Des Moines on their lunch hour. Both officers were fitted for and paid for new suits. The tailor said they would be ready to pick up the following week. Laddie Jobe said he and Ervin received a Saturday morning call from the suit place stating the suits were ready to be picked up. As the officers assigned to serve the search warrants prepared to leave the station and rendezvous, both Jobe and Ervin left the police station at a dash, got in an unmarked detective car and headed "out of the barn" in a hurry to get their new suits. Every media team perched near headquarters were in hot pursuit of these two senior detectives. Ervin looked back and busted out laughing. They arrived at New York Exchange and went in as the press unloaded their equipment from their vehicles. The detectives picked up the suits, thanked the staff and walked out. Reporters waiting outside looked around at each other in silence. Jobe and Ervin passed them saying they were just picking up new suits, got in the unmarked and left. During that time, the real teams left headquarters in various directions undisturbed by the media. They met up at the old grocery store parking lot at 19th and Carpenter to split up into teams and serve the warrants.

The "jump-out squads" executing the search warrants on this case were teams of five detectives, assisted by the tactical unit, and led by a detective sergeant. Teams of uniformed officers provided security outside the residences during the searches. The search warrant for 1517 Washington was executed on Saturday at 6:55 p.m. The team assigned to this warrant was comprised of veteran Sgt. Richard Jones, Detectives Foster, Singleton and Bjornson and Sheriff's Deputy Marshall. An unmarked police vehicle preceded the squads, approached the target house and reported no suspicious or unusual activity around the residence.

No one answered the door when they demanded entry with the search warrant, so they forced the door open with weapons drawn. Singleton went in quickly through the rear door. External security to the perimeter was provided by Officers Oleson, Emary, Terrones, Heller and VanGinkel. Being a two-story house, the team started from the top and searched down. On the second floor, Singleton found a leather holster and letters to Tamara Turner from "Jo-Jo," unknown last name. They confiscated a letter from the Department of Human Services addressed to Anita Jones that verified her residency at that location. There was no one in the house at the time of the search. It was concluded at 7:43 p.m. and items taken were placed in property. None of the suspects were found.

The units assigned to the Carpenter warrant turned the corner approaching the target address and noticed that two young men standing on the sidewalk across the street recognized police vehicles approaching and ran between the houses in the opposite direction. The teams rapidly bailed out and hit the house. Security squads covered the outside area. Detectives identified themselves to the older woman who answered the door and explained that they had a warrant to search the premises. Seeing a dozen police officers taking positions around her house, she reluctantly agreed. Officers scanned the downstairs for any movement and quickly moved to the upstairs area they had been warned about by Sgt. Kail and others. In an upstairs bedroom Rowley and Officer Larry Ihrig found a young black man laying face down, shirtless, on a brown plaid sofa with his arms tucked under him. Intelligence had passed on information developed through Sgt. Dick Kail that a sofa at this residence had a hollowed out arm that might be used to conceal weapons. When the thin black man was ordered to show his hands and get up, he refused. Rowley drew down on him quickly with his 9mm, fearing the suspect may have the Grizzly hidden under him. The suspect exposed his left arm but not his right. Officer Ihrig yelled, "He has something in his hand!" Rowley cocked the 9mm and put it to the man's head, yelling at him to show his other hand NOW! He held it out slowly. He had a nine-inch butcher knife in it that he dropped to the floor. He was forcibly pulled upright at gunpoint by the officers and handcuffed. The first thing that Rowley noticed about him was the gap in his front teeth that Dontrell Ducker had described. He was escorted out of the house in handcuffs. He hollered loudly all the way out, demanding to know what this was all about, claiming he hadn't done anything and wanting a lawyer. He said his name was Joe. The search of the house didn't furnish any productive physical evidence. No guns were found during the search. Alf Freddy Clark was not there. Ident photos were taken of Joe, last name unknown, to add to photo lineups. Joe was then taken to jail.

Detectives then went to an additional house at 1123 24th Street looking for Alf Clark and they were refused admission to the house. Rowley was informed of this development immediately. He and County Attorney Jim Ramey prepared a search warrant. Judge Rodney Ryan read and signed it and a police tactical team hit that house. They searched the house from top to bottom, shaking down all the residents. Clark was not found there but the people there were informed that if they knew where he was, to let him know police would find him and arrest him "one way or another."

Chapter Five

ON THAT EVENING, the 5th of December, Joseph Hodges White, Jr. was interviewed by Lt. Jim Trotter and Detective Ralph Roth after being brought to police headquarters downtown. The interview was conducted in room 317F starting at 8:10 p.m. Present at the interview were Zella Williams, White's great aunt, and Herbert Rogers, an attorney summoned by Mrs. Williams. A juvenile waiver and parental consent form were administered and signed. "Jo-Jo" White was read his rights to which he reluctantly agreed. The interview proceeded from that point:

(Authors note: The following is exact phrasing of statements made by all parties during the interview taken from the official police transcript.)

Roth: This is Senior Police Officer Ralph Roth, Ident #615, taking a statement from Joseph Hodges White, Jr. concerning Des Moines Police Department case number 92-51577, concerning an incident that was reported to the Des Moines Police Department on the 29th of November 1992. Also present is Lt. Trotter from the Des Moines Police Department and also Herbert Rogers, Sr., Attorney at Law and Zella Williams, Joseph White's guardian. For the record, Joseph, could I have your complete name?

White: Joseph Hodges White.

Roth: Is that Joseph Hodges White junior or senior?

White: Junior.

Roth: Joseph, what is your date of birth?

White: October 24, 1975.

Roth: Okay. What is the highest level of education that you've completed?

White: Tenth grade.

Roth: Okay. Where was that at? Where was the last place you attended school, what state was that in?

White: In, um, Seattle, Washington.

Roth: Okay. Was that the current year of 1992 - would be the spring months of 1992?

White: I couldn't - I don't know. It's - it's - I think it was - it might have been in '91.

Roth: All right.

White: Till '92 - somewhere in there. I don't really know, you know, I really ain't good at keeping up on time - real dates from way back there.

Roth: Okay, How long have you been back in the State of Iowa?

White: For about two months.

Roth: And who have you been staying with in those two months?

White: Just - Okay, I was staying with my Uncle Cardell, and now I'm staying with my Aunt Zella. I was just like going back and forth to everybody's house. Here and there but I don't, you know, I remain to stay with my Aunt Zella, you know, off of University.

Roth: Does your Aunt Zella, being Zella Williams, have legal custody of you?

White: Yes.

Roth: All right. And your other uncle, is that Cardell James?

White: Yes.

Roth: Okay. And he lives on the east side of Des Moines? Okay, you're shaking your head, I can't -

White: Yeah, yeah.

Roth: Okay, Do you know where Cardell is living at this time?

White: I don't know the exact street and the name of it, but, yeah, I could take you - I could take you there, but I don't know the name of streets.

Roth: Okay. Are you under any type of medication at this particular point?

White: No.

Roth: Okay. Regarding this case investigation that was opened up by the Des Moines Police Department on the 29th of November 1992, we're talking about an incident which the address is 1111 25th Street in Des Moines. It's called the Drake Diner. And that particular day was a Sunday, which would have been - This is Saturday right now, it would have been a week ago on Sunday. Okay? Can you tell me - I know you said you have a problem with dates or specific things and stuff like that - can you tell me what you did last Sunday?

White: Last Sunday? Me and Freddie - When? The whole day?

Roth: Sure.

White: Okay, well then in the morning we was kicking in, just staying, and we was looking for a ride and we found a ride. So we got the ride and we was driving around. We drove over to this girl's house - I don't know her name, you know, because this was one of his friends, you know what I'm saying? So I really can't, you know, say on that, but we was over at his friend - his girlfriend's house kicking and then about - cause when we came in the house - when we came in the house it was like, I know - I know, cause when I went in the kitchen to get something to eat, you know, every time I go in the kitchen I look at the clock, it was about 6:30 when we came back in the house that night - at night.

Roth: Okay.

White: We stayed over there - well - It seemed like we didn't really leave the house until when it was getting dark, but cause I stayed in the house most of the time and Fred was like running around, you know, he was like running around places and then finally he came and then me and him went over to his girlfriend's house, and we kicked it for a little bit. Then we came home at 6:30, and just stayed there for the rest of the night. Uh - yeah - we stayed there for the rest of the night.

Roth: Okay. When you talk about Freddie, who's Freddie?

White: Freddie Clark.

Roth: Do you know how old a person he is?

White: He's my age.

Roth: Okay.

White: He's seventeen - ain't he seventeen? He's seventeen years old.

Roth: And you say that you'd been together - and was that in the morning time and afternoon time together?

White: We was together in the after - Well we could have left - It seemed like it was dark to me when we left. It was getting towards that point of being dark, but I can't really, you know, say - really put - picture it out, but if we didn't leave close to dark, we must have left - Well, I know we left in the afternoon time, around maybe 3:00, cause we wasn't over at her house for that long. We didn't really do nothing that day, you know. We went over there and drank a little bit, smoked a little bit, and that's it. Then we went back home, so -. We really didn't do nothing that day.

Roth: Okay. How did you get from - Did you leave the house there on Carpenter together? You and Freddie?

White: Uh-huh.

Roth: Okay. And then he went to - You both left there and went to his girlfriend's house?

White: One of his girlfriends.

Roth: One of his girlfriends?

White: Yeah.

Roth: Do you know what that girlfriend's name is?

White: No, not at this point - no. I just met her. I really didn't know the girl.

Roth: Do you happen to know what street you were on?

White: No, I didn't know - I don't really - Cause we had just - I haven't been here for that long, and I really don't be out of the house that much. So, you know, I really don't know all the streets, you know what I'm saying?

Roth: Sure.

White: Yeah, you know, I don't really know all that.

Roth: Can you tell me if she's a white girl or is she a black girl?

White: She's black.

Roth: Do you happen to know how old she is?

White: I don't know. She looked like seventeen or eighteen years old but I don't know. I really don't know the girl.

Roth: But Freddie would know her then, right?

White: Yeah, I think he's - yeah. He took me over there.

Roth: Okay. And while you were there, you said - Did you have - did you drink something?

White: Yeah, we just drunk a beer.

Roth: Just beer?

White: Uh-huh.

Roth: Do you know how much you had?

White: About maybe two cans - two or three cans, cause I don't really drink that much. We just kicked it most of the time. We was getting high though, ya know, smokin'.

Roth: Okay. Were you smoking some weed and stuff like that?

White: Yeah.

Roth: Okay. When you left there - this girl's house that was Freddie's . . . one of his girlfriends -

White: Uh, her name was Tammy.

Roth: Tammy?

White: I think. Yeah - Tammy - I don't know, but I think that's what her name is.

Roth: All right. When you left this girl's house, was it a long
        ways from the house there on Carpenter or was it just
        a short distance?
White: It was a short - it wasn't all that long.
Roth: Okay. When you left there, this girl's house, you stated
        to me that you left there together?
White: Uh-huh.
Roth: Okay. Where did you go after that?
White: To the house.
Roth: Okay. To the house - is that the house on Carpenter?
White: Yeah. I don't know the address but that's where we went.
Roth: Would that be Aunt Zella's house?
White: Yeah, Aunt Zella's house.
Roth: Do you remember who was there at the house when
        you returned?
White: Aunt Zella, Angel, Robert, Chris, and that's about it,
        them four people. All the family was there except for
        Freddie and me. Everybody was there except for
        Freddie and me, all the immediate family.
Roth: And then you and Freddie both returned there?
White: Uh-huh.
Roth: Do you remember what you were wearing that day?
White: I was wearing burgundy pants, burgundy hat, this and
        this, and burgundy pants with some red shoes.
Roth: Okay. Do you remember what -
White: No! No! Not red shoes, some boots - some boots, some
        brown boots.
Roth: Some brown boots?
White: Yeah, they're tan color, yeah.
Roth: Are they canvas or are they tennis shoe type or leather?
White: They're leather. They're high. They're big, they come
        all the way up here. But I let somebody use them,
        somebody else got them right now.
Trotter: (pointing) Okay. You're talking about that sweatshirt -
        you were wearing that shirt, did I understand you to say?

White: Yeah.

Roth: And that hat?

White: Yeah. This and this, and my tan coat. My coat is - I got a big coat that's tan. It's a tan color.

Roth: Okay. Do you remember what Freddie was wearing?

White: Let me see. He was wearing - No, I can't even remember. No. He probably had - I know he had on the 49'ers hat, I know he had on that. And that's all I can remember. Oh, he might have had on his black and gray Nike's too.

Roth: That's shoes then, right?

White: Yeah. And his black pants. I'm thinking black coat. I'm guessing, but I'm pretty sure I'm real close to what - I know he was wearing mostly black - he was wearing mostly all black. He had on a 49'ers coat - I mean a 49'ers hat. I don't know what kind of coat he had on. He might have had his long one on or the red one. I'm pretty - I can't say about the color. I'm not for sure about that.

Roth: Can you remember what your hair style was on that day? Did you have a do-rag on or anything like that? Your hair up or anything?

White (motioning): No, it was this and it was this though.

Trotter: Didn't you tell me a little while ago that you just got your hair cut a couple of days ago?

White: No, just yesterday got it cut.

Trotter: How much did they cut off would you say?

White: (motioning): They cut off about that much.

Trotter: Which would be what - what's your guess? Three or four inches maybe?

White: Something like that.

Trotter: So what you're saying is that it was considerably longer then.

White: Yeah, it was longer than this when they cut it.

Trotter: Okay. Did you have that done in a barbershop?

White: I had it done at uh - I forget the name of the place, but I know -

Trotter: But was it a barbershop?

White: Yeah. it was a shop, yeah.

Roth: What time Sunday did you arrive back at Aunt Zella's house there with Freddie?

White: About 6:30, yeah, it was about 6:30. Cause I went in the kitchen to get something to eat.

Roth: So you looked at the clock there and it said 6:30.

White: Yeah, right there on the front of the stove.

Roth: After you were back there and you went and got something to eat, what did you do that evening?

White: What did we do that evening?

Roth: Yes.

White: Sat in the house, and just looked at TV and whatever, and we was havin fun, you know, talking and just, you know, things you do around the house.

Roth: Did you leave there at all?

White: No.

Roth: Okay. Yourself, did you leave the residence?

White: He did. After he dropped me off, he - let me see -When we came in he stayed there, actually, he did leave again. He left again.

Roth: Do you know where he went?

White: I don't know. But I know he left again, then he came back and that's when the shit came on the news and you know. Cause we was all downstairs when it came on the news, me and Aunt Zella and them guys, and it happened they said it happened at 7:00, and then at when he came in-he came in about - He wasn't gone for that long, so he might have came in either exactly at 7:00 or like maybe 6:50, 6:50 to 7:00 that's when he came in. Cause, you know, I can just figure it out from right here cause I know that he wasn't gone for that long. I know nothing about that. Matter of fact, he did

- he said that he went back over to Tammy's - he went back over to that girl's house, that's where he went to, yeah.

Roth: So when you two went back to the residence there, you're saying Freddie left and came back. How do you know he went back to his girlfriend's?

White: Because I just knew, because when he came back I asked him, I was like, "Where did you go to?" And he was like, "I just went back over there for a minute to talk to somebody."

Trotter: Let's back up just a minute here. Early on when we started this interview, you talked about that particular day you were looking for a ride with somebody, and you said you got a ride with someone, who did you get that ride with?

White: We got it from this lady, and she let us use her car.

Trotter: Oh, I see. You actually took the car, you were driving it yourself. Whose car was it?

White: No, he was - Well, yeah we was driving - yeah we was driving.

Trotter: Whose car was it?

White: I don't even know the lady, he knows her.

Trotter: What kind of car was it?

White: It was a truck.

Trotter: Pickup or van?

White: It wasn't no van, it was a - I don't know. I don't know if it was a pickup or anything either. It was just a truck. A normal old truck. I think it was red or something.

Roth: Okay, Freddie was driving that truck around?

White: Yeah, he was, yeah.

Roth: And you were just riding with him?

White: Yeah.

Roth: Was there anybody else in the truck with you?

White: Uh-huh.

Roth: Who was that?

White: Um, I don't know him, I really couldn't tell you.

Roth: Has he got a street name or anything like that?

White: I think his name is Baby Jay.

Roth: Baby Jay?

White: Yeah, something like that.

Roth: So - I'm trying to get this fresh in my mind. When you left the residence with Freddie the first time, did you walk or drive?

White: When we left the house?

Roth: Uh-huh.

White: We was driving.

Roth: Then you drove over to the girlfriend's house.

White: Yeah.

Roth: All right. And when you left there, you drove -

White: But we went over a lot across the street to get the car. The car was only right across the street from the house, and, you know, the lady lived right across - Well, the lady, she didn't live there, but the one that we know lives there right now and that was her friend. See what I'm saying? And she let us use the car at about - at about - man! - Either it was somewhere around from there - All I could say is from 11 in the -11:00 a.m. to about 3:00 p.m., somewhere around that time period is when we got the car.

Roth: Okay. When you came back to the residence there, which would be Aunt Zella's and Freddie dropped you off - is when you went back to the address there at 2212 Carpenter and you went inside there and you saw the other family members were there and you went in the kitchen, you said it was around 6:30 to get something to eat.

White: Uh-huh.

Roth: Did Freddie just drop you off-you were a passenger in the truck?

White: Yeah, but I was a passenger. I think he came in for a minute.

Roth: Did this Baby Jay, did he come in?

White: Uh-huh. He stayed there with me.

Roth: All right. And then Freddie left and for a short period of time and came back, and you asked him where he had been, and he told you what?

White: He told me that he went back over there - if I'm not mistaken, yeah, I'm pretty sure that's what he said. I'm pretty sure he left and went back over there. I know he did.

Roth: And after he came back to the residence there, you said that you saw something on the news. What was that about?

White: Let me see - if he came in before - I think he came in right before it came on the news or maybe as it was on the news. No, he came in before the news.

Roth: Okay. What do you remember about the news and this particular situation?

White: The news?

Roth: Uh-huh.

White: They said - the Drake Diner had been robbed and two people were shot at. They said the address, I think, of the place or something. I don't know. I really wasn't into the news like all of that. I wasn't like, you know - I was just like, you know, Aunt Zella was looking at it, and we was down there clowning. And, you know, we was talking over the news and stuff and I just happened to glance at it, and it was like two people they said at the Drake Diner, two people were shot. And then I think they gave the address, I don't know. I just know that we seen a little bit of it on TV.

Roth: Okay. Since this - since you saw this on TV and stuff like that, have you had any conversations with anybody about what went on or did you try to find out what went on?

White: No, cause nobody talks, I guess, you know. I asked niggers what was going on about it, but they said they don't know. Everybody said they don't know. They don't know who did it, so I can't answer - I really haven't asked all of them, but I asked a few of them, you know, what's going on. And, like I don't know at the Diner.

Roth: Okay: Did you ever have any conversation with Freddie about it?

White: Yeah. I talked to him about, he said he didn't know what happened either.

Roth: Okay. Do you have - like I said, he's never told you that he did it or anything like that?

White: No.

Roth: Did you ever tell him that you did it?

White: No.

Roth: What do you think should happen to a person that would have been involved in something like that?

White: What do I think should happen to a person that kills?

Roth: Yes.

White: Uh - I guess they should be locked up.

Roth: You think the person deliberately - this is just an opinion, okay, I don't know how else to address it to you. Do you think it was just an accident or the person intended to do it?

Attorney Rogers: I'm going to object to that question. I don't think it's relevant to the investigation.

Roth: Well, again, sir, I'm not going to argue law, I'm just trying to ask him his opinion of what he thought of this particular incident.

White: I don't know. I'm not going to say he did it intentionally or if he did it-I don't know. I mean I wasn't there-see it?

Trotter: Have you ever been in the Drake Diner?

White: I've never been in there, cause I've only been back for about two months. I didn't even know the Drake Diner was there.

Roth: Again, you know, along these particular types of thoughts, can you tell me what you did on Monday?

White: On Monday? Uh - I don't remember. I don't know. I think - we did our thing, sit in the house on the weekdays until maybe night time and then go over to somebody's house. But - yeah - I think we did. I think we went back over - no - I don't know what we did on Monday. I think we just sat in the house cause that's all we do on weekdays. There ain't nothing to do so we just sit in the house.

Roth: Okay. Do you remember what you did on Tuesday?

White: Sat in the house.

Roth: Wednesday?

White: I don't know. Well, Monday and Tuesday we - that's just the everyday thing though, just - but I'm talking about besides, you know, drive - But we only drive around, you know, like going down to Mondamin and stuff, and see who be over there for a little bit, just on the corner talking to people and stuff like that. But that's just an everyday thing - that's an everyday thing. So like Monday, Tuesday, Wednesday, Thursday, Friday, and so if we're not sitting at home all day, then we are out there just talking to them guys on the corners and stuff.

Roth: Okay. When is the last time you've been to the Holiday Inn Central on 6th Avenue?

White: We went there, uh - Wednesday or Thursday.

Roth: Of this last week?

White: Yeah.

Roth: Which room did you stay in?

White: I don't know. I can't remember.

Roth: Who got you the room?

White: Uh - No, I forgot her name. We call her Bunny.

Roth: Who was there with you?

White: Bunny, this other girl, and Tammy, and me, Freddie, and Little Ritchie - Little Ritchie, yeah, that's his name.

Roth: Do you remember if it was a room that you were in or was it a bigger room?

White: It was a room where a door from the other side comes into another room.

Roth: So you had maybe like two rooms or one big room?

White: Uh-huh.

Roth: How long did you stay there?

White: One night.

Roth: How much was the room?

White: $130 - $130 or $140 bucks.

Roth: How was the room paid for?

White: How was the room paid for?

Roth: Yeah.

White: With our money.

Roth: Okay. Do you work anywhere?

White: I just happened to scrape up some money. We're always havin to scrape up money.

Roth: Okay. How much money did you have last week from Monday 'til today?

White: 'Til today? Monday 'til today?

Roth: Right.

White: About $100 - $150, maybe, at the most $150.

Roth: That you, yourself, had.

White: Uh-huh.

Roth: Okay. I understand that most of the time that you're telling me that you just hang around the house because there isn't too much to do in the afternoon until you go out on the street at night and stuff like that. And in that particular time without a place of employment, you could scrape up $150?

White: Where could I scrape it up?

Roth: Yes.

White: That's irregardless of the problem. I got the money. I had the money. And we all had money.

Roth: How much did each of you have to put in for this room?

White: I put in on the room, they bought the beer and the cooler and the pizza and the TV, and just, you know, we just compromised on the room.

Roth: How much money did you have to spend?

White: We already had planned on doing this for a long time, from when I first got here. We all just said, you know, he said that he was going to show me a picnic, and so - I don't - you know - he helped me to get some money and that's what we did. We went to the motel.

Roth: The only girl that you knew there was this Tammy?

White: Yeah, at the most, cause I really don't even really know her. I just, you know, I know that every time I think about it, I can think of her name here and there. Sometimes I can't think of her name.

Trotter: Did you rent the room in your name?

White: Huh-uh.

Trotter: Whose name was it in, do you know?

White: Huh-uh. The girl named Bunny, that's all I know.

Trotter: So there were really three girls there.

White: Yeah, that's what I said.

Trotter: How did you all get down to the Holiday Inn Central? Did you have another car, or borrowed the truck again, or how did you - how did you get down there?

White: This guy gave us a ride.

Trotter: Who? Who was that, do you know who that was?

White: Huh-uh, I don't know who it was. We just asked him could we get a ride to the motel. Cause he came over to her house - came over to her house.

Trotter: Her - meaning?

White: Tammy's house.

Trotter: Tammy's house.

White: Yeah. He came over there, and we asked him for a ride, and it's like get in, you know, no problem. It's all part of the game - same old, same old-doing the same old thing or whatever, Just the same old thing.

Roth: And the only conversation or - like I said - that you've talked to, a couple of people, but they haven't said anything. Have you seen anything else on the news about -

White: Yeah, I see it on the news here and there. Well, we really don't look, we just - you know how they always break off and update you on it, and stuff like that. I watched TV sometimes and they break off of the TV and they like update this, this, this.

Trotter: That Sunday night when you first saw this news report of this incident at the Drake Diner, what were you watching at the time on television, do you remember?

White: We was watching - I couldn't say that - I just know we was watching TV. But we was mostly clowning around, we really wasn't watching, we was just glancing, you know, then it came on. We just glanced at that too, you know. But Aunt Zella was watching, she was into it, but I just glanced at it just for two minutes - or a few seconds maybe.

Roth: Were you downstairs? Watching TV down there?

White: Yeah.

Roth: Do you have a specific room in the house that is your bedroom?

White: Uh-huh.

Roth: Okay. Was that the room the officers got you out of today?

White: Huh-uh. I was in the room where we watch TV at, laying on the couch. And they came, like just - like I didn't know who, it was like, "What the hell is going on," you know. They was like, "We have a search warrant: and this, this and that. I'm like what's happening, whatever.

Roth: Okay.

White: Then they started taking pictures of this, this, and this. Then they said that I didn't have no guardian or something. They said something that's like they said brung me down here or something, man. Then they said they had a search warrant for the house, and they asked me my name and no identification on me.

Roth: In this last week, from the time this incident happened at the Drake Diner until this time here today, had you been at any house or apartment where you saw people that had guns?

White: No.

Roth: Were you at - again, from the time this Drake Diner incident was reported to us until now, at an apartment or a house where a gunshot went off?

White: Huh-uh.

Trotter: Joe, I want you to understand that you're not the only person that we're going to interview about this.

White: I know, but see I'm tired of all these questions.

Trotter: Now listen - just listen, just a minute, now let me finish what I'm saying. Now we're giving you an opportunity here to tell us -

White: Yes.

Trotter: And make sure you don't forget any little detail of things that would have happened, either on Sunday or Monday, or any of the rest of the week. Now is the time for you to talk to us about it. Okay?

White: Uh-huh.

Trotter: And so you really got to think real hard and concentrate on those particular days.

White: I had forgot all about the motel, to tell you the truth. Cause that like I said, I don't really be thinking all that hard, I just be like - you know - It's because of - I mean, it's not like I was trying to hide anything. I'll tell you straight up. All he had to do was say it in the first place and I would have -

Trotter: Well, I understand, I just wanted to make sure that there aren't some other things, you know, along the line that you haven't forgotten about. So think real hard when

Detective Roth asks you these questions, and make sure you concentrate real hard and remember exactly the things that happened on those nights about being at any other location and maybe guns being seen or accidentally fired, or whatever. Think real hard about that. Okay?

White: Yeah, somebody was in the house - we was all in the house, and somebody had a gun and I asked if I could see it, you know, and I accidentally shot the gun on the floor.

Trotter: Where was this now? Was this at Zella's you mean?

White: Tammy's, whatever the girl's name is - Tammy or whatever.

Trotter: Okay. What night was that? When was that?

White: It was - I don't know, I can't tell you. I don't really - you know - that's what I'm saying. I have to - If you tell me - if you say - then I could think, you know, a little bit more about it, and I could say whether it was day or night. You know what I'm saying?

Roth: Just take your time and think about it. The Drake Diner was on Sunday, and it could have been - and you know, it doesn't make any difference to me that you were at the hotel. Try to concentrate, like I said, between the time of the Drake incident to the time that you went to the motel - or the hotel, about being at Tammy's house and who was around there. It was a foolish thing like you were telling me that, you know, that you asked somebody to look at a gun and it went off. Who had been around there at that time, and also who had the gun and stuff like that. We're not out to get people with that. Just think about it - about that incident, Okay?

Trotter: I want to remind you again, it's extremely important, this is a very - probably the most important thing that is ever going to happen in your life to date is this interview right now. Now is the time to start thinking and concentrate on all of these events that we're talking about. Now I know it's tough, because you had no reason to remember it, you know - why remember it. Now there is a reason, so you really need to think hard and remember that this is a serious matter.

White: I know, but -

Trotter: Now listen just one more second.

White: What's the motel got to do with all this?

Trotter: That's not what I'm talking about, the motel. I'm not talking about the motel. I'm talking about this accident that you had with that gun.

White: What? Where it accidentally went off?

Trotter: Yes.

White: Well, what? What you want to know?

Trotter: Well, we've already asked you what night. You got to think real hard, what night did it happen?

White: Ah-shit. Wednesday, Thursday - shit. Wednesday, Thursday, I don't know. I know it was maybe one of them two nights.

Trotter: Wednesday or Thursday.

White: Yeah. I think it might have been Wednesday.

Trotter: And you say it was at Tammy's house. Who else was there?

White: Little Jay, Baby Jay, and me, Freddie, Tammy, Bunny, and Sharona.

Trotter: What was that last name you gave me?

White: Sharona, Sharonia.

White: I think maybe that's about it. I'm not for sure though, there could have been more people. Everybody was running in and out - sort of like that. Everybody was running in and out.

Trotter: Partying?

White: No, not really partying, but getting high, you know, just the same thing that we do over there all the time. That's how I - that's when I asked him and stuff if I could see the gun and it accidentally went off cause I was high.

I was like "Can I see it?"- and I was playing with it, and I dropped my hand like this cause somebody said something to me, and I was like, "What?" I looked at them like that and it just - as I dropped it, it fell - the thing went down on my hands "POW" I said, get it away from me, you know what I'm saying? Then we left cause they started tripping saying the police was going to be there. So they told us to leave, actually, cause we was going to stay here.

Trotter: So when you left, you left with whom? Of all these people that you told me about, did you leave with just one or two of them or all of them, or -

White: Freddie. I think it was the same night we went to the motel. I don't know man, I'm confused. It wasn't -

Roth: Okay. I'm just trying to play this back. He said he accidentally discharged his gun. Okay, do you know if it was a big gun or a small gun? Do you know the difference between an automatic, or a semi-automatic, and a revolver?

White: It was a revolver. It was a .44 revolver.

Roth: A .44?

White: Or a .38. It was a .38 Special revolver or a .44 revolver. I really wasn't sure cause I was just, you know, playing. I wasn't really like - You know what I'm saying?

Roth: Yeah.

White: And then somebody happened to call me as I just started playing with it. I was like, "What?" and "BAM." I'm like, "Oh, here, take it."

Roth: Are you right or left handed?

White: I'm left handed. I'm like, what-I'm both handed really.

Roth: Ambidextrous?

White: I can use my right hand too, only I can use my left hand just as good as I can with my right hand.

Roth: Okay. This weapon that you were talking about - I was trying to ask you if you could determine or if you

could remember if it was either a dark colored finish
or a dark blue finish versus what I call like a chrome
finish or a nickel plated, which is very light frame.

White: I think it was blue steel.

Roth: Okay. And it discharged only one time?

White: Yeah.

Roth: Okay. Whereabouts in this residence were you at in this
girl's house?

White: Where were we?

Roth: Yeah. Was it in the front room, bathroom, or bedroom
when this happened?

White: I don't know - the bedroom - I don't know. It was the
kitchen. Yeah, it was in the kitchen, yeah. Or maybe it
was in the dining room - I don't know. I was high, I was
messed up, you know. And all I know is that I had some
type of gun in my hand for a moment, you know,
and "POW."

Roth: Okay. When you left that residence with Freddie, was
that weapon with you or was it left behind?

White: It was left behind. It wasn't ours.

Roth: Okay. When you saw this gun at this house - at Tammy's
house there, were other people playing with it or
something like that? What intrigued you about it, why
did you want to see the gun?

White: Because he had - he was playing with it for the moment.
And I asked him if I could see it.

Roth: Okay. Since last Sunday - Okay - when this incident
happened at the Drake Diner until this time, have you
had - have you been stopped by the police in any way?

White: Yeah, in the car. I think we was stopped, but they didn't
ask no names, they just asked the driver for the driver's
license. I think about two times - two or three times.

Roth: Okay. And like I said, you weren't driving so they didn't
ask your name or anything like that.

White: No.

Roth: Joseph, again, I just kind of want this kind of etched in stone so I can have a perception of what we've been talking about here. The incident at the Drake Diner was on a Sunday, and in your statement here that you were home at 6:30, was back kind of joking around the house there and there was kind of a news flash came on and stuff like that, and you're telling me that you didn't leave the residence at all.

White: After 6:30, no.

Roth: Okay. But there was an opportunity that Fred had - Freddie left for a little bit and he got back home.

White: He only left for about thirty minutes, man, at the most. I really don't know, but I know he wasn't gone for that long. And I know he wouldn't do it to - I hope not. I mean, man, I know cause he's like me, you know. He wants to do something like get a job - you know what I'm saying? It ain't even worth it, so I just try to get me a job now. Matter of fact, today he was looking for a job. So I know he wouldn't do it either. You know what I'm saying? He wouldn't do it either. I know he wouldn't. I hope he he didn't cause - I doubt it.

Roth: Did you hope that he wouldn't do it, you doubt he did it and stuff like that. He hasn't come out and said to you, being Freddie, that he made a mistake and it was an accident. He was involved in this situation up at Drake.

White: No.

Roth: Okay. The only knowledge that you have about that incident at Drake Diner is what you've heard either from TV or from what people have said to you?

White: People haven't said anything. Well, some people say just like a few things about it, but nobody said no names or nothing - they never say no names, they just be like we all know who did it, but we got ideas, you know, but they don't ever tell nobody, they just - whoever was talking about it they just keep it between themselves. So they must have heard something from somebody and they just keep to themselves, you know what I'm saying?

Roth: Like I said, in the time that you were at this girl's house when you accidentally discharged that weapon into - what - the floor area, is that where it was, or was it the ceiling?

White: It was in the floor. Cause I said something and "POW" and I was like "Take this mother fucker." You know, here, I don't want it - I don't need this gun.

Roth: Okay. I understand. Joseph, it's kind of hard for me to comprehend this particular - The reason why, you know, that we're talking to you about this investigation is because the weapon that fired that round into that floor was also used in the Drake Diner crime.

White: Was it?

Roth: Absolutely, it was.

White: But they said on the TV that the one -

Roth: That TV doesn't know what we know about that particular deal, okay? That particular weapon that discharged into the floor at the residence up there where this girl lives, okay? That you accidentally did it, that weapon has been scientifically - okay - linked to the Drake Diner. So that's why I'm saying, you know, it's pretty hard for me and Lt. Trotter, and also I believe with Mr. Rogers here that we're trying our best to understand that - I know it's hard to give somebody up - okay? - but what you have to understand is that weapon - you have knowledge or that person. That person, again, might be involved or might not be involved. But we have to know who you got that particular weapon from and where did it go?

White: And where did it go?

Roth: Yeah.

White: It went right back into his hand.

Roth: Can you describe him?

White: He's about 5'5" or 5'8", somewhere in there.

Roth: Do you know that person's name or initials?
           (Silence)

Trotter: You've got to remember what I was telling you a little
           while ago. This is -

White: So what man, I'm not saying his name cause that would
           be wrong - that would be wrong. I ain't going to sit up
           here and say that name. As long as I know that I didn't
           do it, I don't care. I don't care what you - I ain't saying
           nothing about nobody, I don't care.

Trotter: Do you think that someone else, if we go out and run
           some of these other folks down, what do you think they
           will tell us?

White: Maybe. I don't know. You got to go talk to them.

Trotter: Do you think they'll recount this story basically the way
           you told it?

White: Yeah.

Trotter: About this happening on Wednesday night?

White: I don't know if it happened on Wednesday night.

Roth: What I'm saying and I think what Lt. Trotter is trying
           to say is, you know, if these other people were talked
           to or interviewed, you think or you hope that they would
           tell it the same way.

White: They can come in and say whatever they want to say.

Roth: I would not want to be involved, you know, linked into
           this thing where those people are out there. Money is a
           motivating factor, they could come up with all the
           hair-brained stuff in the world, and I can say, Hey, when
           Joseph White came in, we talked to him about this
           particular deal. He told us each and everything we
           needed to know about it. I'm not here to judge, I'm not
           here to do that. I'm just trying to get some information
           that you told me about. Okay?

White: I don't know who - That might not have been him, you know, that did the shooting. He might not have had the gun.

Trotter: If that person doesn't have that gun now, and maybe somebody gave it to them and you just didn't see it. But we need to know that so we can go to them and say, Where did you get it or what did you do with it? You see, that's the key to this whole thing, is trying to track that gun.

Attorney Rogers: Why can't you use the information that he's given you already and track it down. He's already described this individual.

Roth: This tall?

White: I said he's about 5'8".

Roth: How old a person is he?

White: I ain't going to say that either.

Roth: See!

White: Cause that's - man, man, man. That's the only thing - that you would be satisfied?

Roth: Yeah. If I knew who this person was.

White: No. I'm not talking about how old he was. I'm not going to - you know that, man. That would be wrong for me to do that.

Roth: No. Wrong? It was like - That's that person's problem. My thing is, you picked this thing up, and said, Hey, look at this thing, and "BOOM," that's that person's responsibility, you know.

White: I don't know all that.

Trotter: We're honest with you, because we're telling you that that gun IS the gun. There's no question. There's no other gun anywhere else. That's the gun that was involved in the Drake Diner incident. See. That's the bad thing here. It's not like we're talking about somebody stole a gun in a house prowl, that's not what we're talking about.

White: His name is David.

Trotter: What? David? I want to tell you right now, and I'm
         sure Mr. Rogers is going to tell you, you have done the
         correct thing.

Roth: You know David's last name?

White: I don't know that.

Trotter: Well, which one of these people here is David?
         Old Jay, Baby Jay, Thomas - ?

White: He's not none of them.

Trotter: He was an additional person that was there then? David?

Roth: How old is David?

White: He's about sixteen.

Roth: He's pretty young, isn't he?

Trotter: Fifteen or sixteen, you say?

White: He's about sixteen.

Roth: Do you know where he lives?

White: I just know that I seen him over there, but I've seen
         him up over by the school and I've seen him over there.

Roth: Is he as tall as you are?

White: Huh?

Roth: Is he taller than you or is he shorter than you?

White: He's shorter than me.

Roth: Okay. You're what - 5'8" or 5'9"?

White: I'm about 5'9", no, I'm 5'10" maybe.

Roth: Is he big frame or small frame?

White: Who? Him?

Roth: Yeah.

White: He's about 5'8". He's built about like me, sort of.
         He's about my coloring.

Roth: Does he have any moustache or beard or goatee or
         anything like that?

White: No - Yeah, I think he had a moustache. Yeah, he's got a
         moustache, he's got a moustache.

Roth: And his name is David?

White: Yeah, I don't know. I don't know all that. I just know that I've seen him a few times, and I happened to see him there.

Trotter: How was he carrying it? Did he have it in a holster?

White: Huh?

Trotter: Was it stuck in his pants or something?

White: Yeah.

Roth: And you said it was, again, a revolver, which means it has a cylinder in it.

White: Yeah, it was one of those.

Trotter: Did it kick shells out when it fired?

White: It didn't kick no shell out, just "POW".

Roth: Okay. But I think it's even been reported in the news that this particular weapon, that there was evidence left behind there. And that's why I'm saying what a revolver looks like. That's what you're telling us. If you're confused about what a semi-automatic looks like - do you know what a .45 looks like?

White: That's a 9 millimeter.

Trotter: Well, forget about what caliber it is, did it look like that?

White: Yeah. But it wasn't no Grizzly.

Roth: You know a Grizzly?

White: Huh? No. I seen it on the news though. I seen that gun that was on the news, it wasn't one of them.

Roth: That you had.

White: That he had.

Roth: That this David had?

White: It was a - I wasn't really looking at it like that though. I'm pretty sure it was a Desert Eagle, because I heard him saying something about it earlier. I just can't - I heard him say Desert Eagle.

Trotter: Was that something that you heard from David or - you didn't actually read it on the gun.

White: No, I didn't actually read it on the gun. But it seems, but you know they had it on - But a Grizzly - but that ain't the same one cause it don't look nothing like that gun. It doesn't look like that gun. I mean I did look at it for a minute, but I wasn't reading it like - you know what I'm saying and stuff?

Trotter: Yeah, I understand. So after the shot, where did David go?

White: We all left. And he left, he went his own way - he went his own way. He didn't want to come with us.

Trotter: He evidently lives in that area do you think, or - ?

White: He does live back there in those houses. The house is in the back, I think. I'm not for sure, he might have got an aunt or someone that lives back there.

Trotter: Have you seen this fella since that night?

White: No. But I don't think he did it.

Trotter: How come?

White: Cause I don't think he'd do it. Well, you know, I'm just saying who had the gun. I didn't say that he, you know, did that murder cause I don't know, you know, I don't know.

Roth: Well, we know that.

White: Cause he could have probably bought it from somebody, you know. And plus, you know, I seen the gun I mean, and it didn't look like the gun that was on TV.

Roth: You mentioned Grizzly. Where did that come from?

White: I seen it on TV.

Roth: Okay. Is there anything else about this that's coming back to you or anything like that?

White: Coming back to me?

Roth: Yes, or remembering any other incidents where you might have been around where there were guns?

White: No.

Roth: Is there anything that you can think of that can help us in this investigation?

White: No. No. Cause don't nobody know nothing about it.

Roth: Rest assured that I can tell you right here and today that that weapon is the weapon, Okay?

Trotter: And since the night the gun accidentally discharged - since that night that the gun that you had in your hand went off, have you seen that gun since?

White: No, I haven't.

Attorney Rogers: Can we conclude this?

Trotter: I just wanted to make sure he hasn't thought of something else. Don't be afraid to tell us. Now's the time to get it off your chest. Understand that we may never be able to talk like this again. You feel comfortable that you've told us everything that you know about this, then?

White: Well, I feel like I don't have to worry about the police being on my back anymore. Cause I know everybody's getting dragged in, you know, so everybody, you know - I was going to come down here on my own, but I just - I didn't really want to come and do that cause, you know, this trouble and you know what I'm saying, man?

Roth: When were you going to come down and see us about this?

White: Huh?

Roth: When were you going to come down and see us about this?

White: I said I was going to, yeah, I was going to, but then I started thinking about it, I was like, you know - cause then, you know, they going to get the wrong ideas. You know how - I know you just the investigators and all, and you know sometimes - you be thinking, Oh, well if he knows something about it then he must - I mean you must have been involved in it, or you could have did it, or, you know, you might have got someone in mind, you know, and stuff like that. And I ain't got no time for all that shit and stuff. That's why I was having second thoughts on it, but I was going to have her come down here with me, so she could bring that paper in -

that paper saying that she's in my custody and just come down here and say few things about it, you know. Then just leave it at that anyway.

Roth: Okay. Is the information that you've given here today, and this evening, this particular statement, the truth to the best of your knowledge?

White: Yeah, to the best of my knowledge, yeah.

Roth: Myself as being a police officer and Lt. Trotter being a police officer - have I threatened you or coerced you to make this particular statement?

White: No.

Roth: Is this statement that you have made here today to us, freely and voluntarily?

White: Yes.

Trotter: I don't have any more questions.

Attorney Rogers: Is he free to go then?

Trotter: The County Attorney is the one that will make those decisions.

Roth: This interview is concluded at 22:35 hours on the 5th of December. Thank you.

Joseph White Jr. remained in custody. Alf Freddy Clark, knowing that the police were after him, turned himself in at police headquarters later the same night shortly before 10:00 p.m..

Joseph "Jo-Jo" White, Jr.

Chapter Six

ON SUNDAY morning, December 6th, *The Des Moines Register* readers awoke to the headline "Teens held in diner slayings". The story said that no charges had been filed but police said one juvenile was a suspect and the other "a material witness *at least.*" [9] Sgt. Ray Rexroat addressed the media with the news saying that the suspects would be turned over to juvenile authorities. However, he would not say where they were being held. A woman interviewed by TV news, who would not give her name, but said she was one of the youth's grandmothers, said, "They are just trying to railroad him because his name is Joseph White, Jr."

The press sought out attorney Herbert Rogers. Rogers told them, "From my participation and questioning, I don't believe they (the police) have the right suspect or witness." He said the way the interview went, he didn't think the information provided would incriminate anyone. "We're just waiting to see what course the county attorney's office will take. After reading the paper today and participating, the only question I have is when they are going to be released." Reporters asked Rogers if he had been retained as the lawyer for the two and he said he had not. He said that he had been asked by Ako Abdul Samad of the Urban Dreams organization right after the arrests to sit in on the interview [10].

Later on, at a Sunday press conference, Lt. Jobe said that police heard nothing they didn't expect to hear in the interview and that they weren't disappointed in what the two 17-year-old suspects said. Jobe said the motive was robbery and the gunman took between $400 and $500 from the cash register. Reporters asked if the crime had anything to do with gangs. Jobe said, "There is nothing to indicate this had anything to do with gangs." Reporters continued and asked if the teenagers were street gang members. Jobe said, "No comment." [11] Police did not release their identities to the media and they just referred to them as juveniles. They were identified by name to the media by relatives.

Detective Dennis Westover and his crew remained convinced that Alf Freddy Clark was the real killer. They had the new photo of Joseph White, Jr. that Ident took of him at the time of his arrest. They added it to a photo lineup that also contained a photo of Freddy Clark - among others. They made contact with Scott Birrer, who they considered to be the most reliable eyewitness. Scott agreed to look at the photo lineup. Much to the surprise of the investigators, he picked out Jo-Jo White. Westover contacted Lt. Jobe and told him the focus of the investigation had shifted to a new suspect. They showed the same photo lineup to Dontrell Ducker and he told them White was the shooter. They asked him if he was sure. He said that he went to school with Joe White. He recognized him on the night of the shooting.

Agent Doug Fagan of the DCI looked puzzled and asked Jim Rowley about the buzz he heard about Jo-Jo White's father. He didn't have a clue what they were referring to. Rowley grimaced, sighed and said, "Jo-Jo White *Senior* was wanted for rape and attempted murder for raping a teenage girl in Witmer Park and beating up her boyfriend. Officers Mike Nehring and Jim Osterquist stopped him and another guy at 17th and Crocker in 1977. They were responding to a call that two women were being harassed there. Before the officers could put together who they had, White emptied a .357 magnum into the two officers and nearly killed them. Osterquist, badly wounded, managed

to get shots off at Jo-Jo White – hit him in the back and killed him. We found White in an alley almost a block away, flat on his face with the gun still in his hand. Jo-Jo *Senior* had a wife and four kids. Jo-Jo White *Junior* was one of the four kids. And, Alf Freddy Clark, Jo-Jo's cousin – his father spent three years in the joint for attempted murder and manslaughter for killing a 17 year-old girl and seriously wounding her boyfriend. The acorn apparently doesn't fall far from the tree."

    ON MONDAY morning, juvenile section officers and juvenile court officers confirmed that Joseph Hodges White, Jr. had no criminal record in Des Moines. They took the additional step of contacting Nancy Wilson, staff supervisor of the juvenile division of the King County, Washington Prosecutor's Office. She said that Jo-Jo White had been convicted of six felonies and three misdemeanors between August 1990 and October of 1991. The convictions included 2ⁿᵈ degree burglary, 2ⁿᵈ degree possession of stolen property and 3ʳᵈ degree assault. She added that two warrants were still pending for him in Washington State for failure to appear on theft charges and failure to appear on a felony assault charge. ¹²

    JO-JO WHITE was formally charged with 1ˢᵗ degree murder and 1ˢᵗ degree robbery on Tuesday morning. Polk County Attorney John Sarcone requested to have the trial moved to adult court. George Arvidson, chief attorney for the juvenile division of the public defender's office was initially appointed White's lawyer with John Wellman counseling. Attorney John Wellman, well-known successful defender of the indigent and the underprivileged, was taking notice of the legal proceedings concerning White and making his feelings known to authorities and the media. He told Detective Rowley that he was convinced "they arrested the wrong kid." Wellman wanted to move right on to trial without further delay to get it over with.

A few of the detectives assigned to the Drake Diner investigation were now being released from the case and re-assigned to their regular duties due to the overload of other cases and investigations. Those detectives still working on the case continued to accumulate information, reporting and tracking records of .44 LAR Grizzlys. Jim Rowley re-interviewed Barbara Hogan who provided further information concerning the truck that Alf Freddy Clark and Jo-Jo White "borrowed" the day of the murders. She described the truck as a red Chevy type pickup, but she was not real sure of the make. She indicated that it did have a topper on it. She also said the white woman who owned the truck went by the name "Smoker," indicating she was a druggie. Other reports received indicated that Alf Freddy Clark gave her crack cocaine to borrow the truck.

Detective Singleton followed up on lead #260 which came in prior to Jo-Jo White's arrest. It was an anonymous Crime Stopper lead concerning Joseph White, Jr. of 2212 Carpenter. The caller described him physically, said that he wore a black cap and that he was a member of the CRIPS gang and an associate of Alf Freddy Clark. The caller stated that she was at 2212 Carpenter with several gang members around Thanksgiving when she saw a long handgun. She also heard Joseph White saying that he had robbed the 7-Eleven store with that particular gun. Since it was an anonymous lead, it was of little additional value beside the fact that it made reference to facts already established.

Detective Ralph Roth and Sgt. Bernie Taylor of the West Des Moines Police Department were teamed together. On Monday, December 7th, they spoke with Jo-Jo White's girlfriend. She confirmed Joe's involvement in an earlier 7-Eleven robbery. This information was forwarded to Des Moines Detective Doug Harvey who was investigating that crime.

When asked his reaction to the Drake Diner murders by the press, Polk County Sheriff Bob Rice said it was tragic and that he opposed large handguns. "I don't think we need these big handguns out there on the street. There's no reason for it. A person should have the right to protect his home and family, but some of these guns are just too big to do anybody any good. They shouldn't be out there." [13]

During the press briefing on Tuesday, December 8th, police were asked when they began to focus on Jo-Jo White. They said his name came up a day or two after the crime was committed. When asked about the evidence that the police had implicating White, police officials refused to comment but added that the evidence would probably become public following the January 5th hearing. They did say they were investigating the connection between Clark and White and the Vice Lords street gang. Media representatives asked what charges had been filed against Alf Freddy Clark. Investigators said it was just parole violation at that time. They asked why and for what reason parole violation. Police said that he had admitted his involvement with the Vice Lords gang, which was a violation of the terms of his parole: Actually there was a little more to it. Juvenile court officer Gwen Lewis requested the court consider revoking his parole and placing him in the state training school at Eldora for four violations of his parole:

- Use of alcohol and marijuana on December 1st at the all night party at the Holiday Inn.
- Association with other delinquents including Jo-Jo White.
- He was known to have been in possession of a weapon.
- His admission to police during interrogation of being involved with the Vice Lords.

Clark's record included charges in July of 1990 of 1st degree robbery, which was dismissed, and attempted murder, which was reduced to 1st degree terrorism.

THREE RELATIVES of the two suspects called a Wednesday
news conference at the West Side Athletic Club, just north of
downtown Des Moines. Zella Berry, Jo-Jo White's aunt; Dora
James, White's grandmother and Clark's great aunt; and Zella
Williams, Alf Freddy Clark's mother and White's great aunt,
wanted "to show the other side" of the two youths and announce
that a legal defense fund had been established in their behalf at
WestBank in West Des Moines.

Speaking to newsmen, Dora James said, "It was a cruel
murder. Whoever did it had to be a terribly sick person. But I
do not believe these boys are guilty." Bathed in the glare of the
television lights, the three women calmly faced a contingent of
reporters and photographers. The statements were accompanied
by the sound of fists slamming into punching bags in the
adjacent room of the athletic club. The women said that they
feared that the large reward offered for the arrest may have led
people to provide false information. James said, "The money
is out there and it's tempting to a lot of people." They said that
they did not believe that either could receive a fair trial in Des
Moines. They feared that attempts to quickly pass the death
penalty could affect both boys if convicted. They said that both
youths are being judged, at least partially, on the past reputations
of some family members.

Zella Berry said, "These are two innocent boys. Treat them
right." When she heard mention of the death penalty, she said,
"You're looking at your nephew and your cousin in the electric
chair." Dora James added that she thought the "kids were being
railroaded." Zella Williams said that both youths were high
school dropouts but they had been making plans to continue
their educations. She had been trying to make arrangements
to enroll Joseph White in school here. She continued that she
hadn't seen White for several years until he returned but she
characterized him as "a pretty sweet child". She did acknowledge
however that "he had his problems" including a long police
record in Seattle. When asked about her son, Alf Freddy Clark,

she called him "very sensitive" and "a good kid." Though she did say that he had been involved with gangs. [14]

As the TV crews began unplugging their equipment, someone asked the three if they had anything else they wanted to say. Zella Berry looked up and said, "People need to pray. This is a cruel world and it gets crueler every day."

THE SEARCH for the murder weapon continued. The pressure was on for a break in this case based on the lengthy process of finding each Grizzly .44. As the number of Grizzlys confirmed grew, police began to wonder what the next step would be if this search went sour. Long hours of phone calls and teletypes were not paying off. Supervisors began double-checking the results and that annoyed the detectives who had spent their usual days off working on the phones with local law enforcement personnel and gun dealers in their assigned states.

Singleton, like the others, saw immediately when this search began that he was going to have to enlist the assistance of local law enforcement in his assigned states to verify these weapons. Phone calls were made to the police jurisdictions where the guns were shipped. Local officers were assigned who would be responsible for making contact with the individual gun shops. The lists would involve a lot of work to verify and complete. In the case of the Wild Road Gun Shop in Manitee, Michigan, the assigned officer's name was Trooper Ray Keifer. Detective Singleton sent the following communication to Keifer that was typical of the messages relayed concerning the investigation:

To: Michigan State Police
Attn: Trooper Ray Keifer ID# MI510770

Currently following up on a double homicide occurred in our city on 29 Nov 92. Weapon used was a Grizzly Mark IV .44 magnum. We are contacting all gun shops that ATF states had this weapon sent to them.

I would appreciate your assistance in checking the Wild Road Gun Shop, 635 Wild Road, Manitee, MI 49660. A Grizzly Mark IV .44 Magnum S/N – F000379 was shipped to them on 02 Apr 92.

What I would like to know is if they still have the weapon or, if they sold it to somebody else: I need name, address + phone number of buyer.

You may either call me at 515-284-4868 or Teletype back to DMPD.

Many of the Grizzlys were still in the gun shops awaiting sale. Several were sold though. The owners were contacted and reports back to Des Moines detectives typically were:

Michigan State Police
12/15/92 1330 Grizzly sold to:

Leonard T. Marcus
15860 Wall Street
Melvindale, MI 48122
Non-published phone

12/16/92 1445 Lt. Smithson made contact with Marcus. He still has weapon - S/N verified.

Businesses in the State of Alaska took delivery on several Grizzlys. The handgun was well suited to the rigors of the territory and the wildlife encountered there. Jim Rowley had work to do to locate these far away weapons. Seven guns went to the Great Northern Gun Shop in Anchorage. One Grizzly went to Sky Line Sales, also in Anchorage. Twelve guns went to Boon Docks Sporting Goods at the corner of Horse Shoe and Eagle River Loop in Eagle River, Alaska. Three guns went to Down Under Distributors in Fairbanks. Two guns went to the Western Auto Store in Juno. Detective Rowley contacted this long list of businesses, such as Gun & Ammo Shop on Turpin Road in Anchorage: They had one Grizzly shipped to them – serial number F000103. They sold the weapon to John Vance in Wasillia, Alaska. Rowley contacted Mr. Vance and he still had the gun. After all, each owner had to be contacted and each weapon accounted for.

Detective Rowley talked with several gun stores and individuals that had the guns in their possession. Contact could not be made with some registered owners, so Rowley sent teletypes to the Eagle River Police, the Anchorage Police and the Alaska State Highway Patrol requesting their assistance in finding those guns that were unaccounted for. All agencies contacted replied that the firearms in question had been located and accounted for.

Detective Bill Boggs had fifteen Grizzlys to locate in the State of Washington. Seven were in the King County, Washington area, which includes Seattle and the surrounding communities. King County is geographically the largest county in the country covering 220 square miles. Boggs personally made several calls and had to enlist the help of the King County Sheriff's Office to complete the task of accounting for all of the guns in their area. King County obliged and said they would get back to him.

Federal Alcohol, Tobacco and Firearms agents made it clear to Des Moines' investigators that any gun owner or shop that refused to cooperate would be "dealt with" by ATF accordingly. Typically, owners or possessors of Grizzly .44 Magnums were owners (or sellers) of several guns. A close review of records and practices of shops, and/or owners, of many firearms by the government was not what anyone of sound mind would welcome. Additionally, pressure was on to find the weapon used in the crime. They thought that the weapon might be involved in another incident of some sort and they could recover it and trace it back to the diner. Local hoods were feeling the pressure to find the gun. Traffic stops and shakedowns were stepped up under orders from Chief Moulder. The police made it clear that the person who found this gun would be in a pretty good bargaining position relating to themselves and their situation.

On December 11th, burglars broke into the home of Phyllis Burnett at 1450 Dean Avenue. They stole a video recorder, thirty movies, jewelry and money. Most important to Phyllis, they took homemade videotapes, some of which contained footage of her son Tim who had been killed.

The Polk County Attorney's Office was involved in daily meetings with investigators concerning the Drake Diner. They felt that the case was still weak from a conviction standpoint. Steve Foritano emphasized that Polk County juries could not be depended upon to convict on evidence that police and prosecutors were convinced of, but left room for speculation and disagreement in the jury chambers.

Jim Rowley was concerned. He was preoccupied with finding the murder weapon. He also told Rick Singleton that there were "just too many loose ends in the case" - even with Jo-Jo White in jail. Jim had lost in court before but never on a scale approaching the fallout from an acquittal on this. He'd lay awake at night, even after the long, exhausting work days. It was a source of concern for his wife Connie.

Chapter Seven

THE DES MOINES REGISTER finally reported the aftermath of events of the crime on Thursday, December 17th with a front-page headline story "Slaying suspects spent loot on party." "While relatives grieved for victims of Drake Diner shooting, investigators believe the gunman held a bash at a local hotel." The police department was officially releasing nothing that would hinder or compromise the investigation, but the Register reported: "The two police sources who described the hotel party did so on condition that *they would not be identified.* [15] They declined to say whether the party was related to White's arrest and would not provide details."

Following that leak, reporters turned to Police Chief Moulder to elaborate. He told them that police would not discuss strategies and details of the investigation. Reporters searched out detectives who had been assigned to the case and asked about Alf Freddy Clark's role in the crime. The detectives would not budge. The media found out through 'unauthorized sources' about the discharge of the gun at Anita Jones' residence. The press hurried over and interviewed Anita Jones who said that now the media was saying there was a connection between the gun fired into her floor and the one in the diner. She added that one of her children had been running with the Vice Lords for some time and, although she was away when the shot was fired, she believed gang members were the ones responsible.

Police remained mum about evidence in the case. Spokesman Sgt. Ray Rexroat said that he would not answer questions about the shooting at the house but he did provide copies of the police report - edited in spots with grease pencil. Search warrants containing probable cause and lists of items seized remained secret. A hearing had been requested and set for the following Wednesday to determine if search warrants should be made available to the public. The Polk County Attorney's Office claimed in court that release of these search warrants would jeopardize continuing police investigations, in spite of the fact that an arrest had already been made.

THE POLICE DEPARTMENT was doing its best to enforce a gag order on leaks in the case. Police supervisors again told all department personnel that the release of information related to the Drake Diner murder case was NOT authorized and would result in severe disciplinary action against anyone involved, including possible termination. Without many new details to release, the Register turned their attention to what was considered a related story: "Gun permit requests rise after 2 slayings." The number of requests jumped to 67 in the week following the slayings compared to 39 the week before. Many people said the slayings played a role. David House, 32, a mechanic at Noble Ford Mercury, a car dealership in Indianola just south of Des Moines, said the diner slayings helped him justify the permit to his wife who's scared to death to have a gun in the house. "I feel it's my responsibility to protect myself and my family." [16]

After her sister was slain at the Drake Diner, Molly McGrane, 27, a nursing student urged people to boycott stores that sell guns. She said the increase in permit applications is "exactly the opposite of what I'd like to see happen." [17]

NEARLY THREE WEEKS after the murders, an interview was arranged with Jo-Jo White's mother, Sharon James.

It was conducted in the office of her attorney Don Nickerson. Attending were Jim Rowley and Assistant County Attorney Jim Ramey. The interview lasted about 45 minutes and was taped by both Rowley and Nickerson. Sharon James said that she and her son, Joseph Hodges White, lived in Kent, Washington, a suburb of Seattle. They lived at 712 Waterman, Building "D", Apartment 105. She said that she drove her son to Des Moines on the 9th of November, 1992 and left him with his great aunt, Zella Williams. After a short stay in town she returned to Washington State, only to return when she heard about Joseph's trouble.

She was emphatic about the circulating stories that someone else had committed the murders. Her first account was that she heard somebody named "Jay" did it. According to her, he supposedly lived on 22nd Street and had a blue car. Police knew that she was referring to Jay Spenser (who was not a suspect any longer as a result of the investigation). She said that her family told her that Joe was at home in his shorts, not dressed when the shootings occurred. Then she combined that with an account of running into a little girl, who she did not know, who'd been at the 2212 Carpenter residence. The girl said that she had been there following the shootings and Joe didn't have any money when she asked him for money. Sharon James went on to say that somebody, who she didn't know, told her that Joe was set up by gang members because Freddy Clark had been told to get rid of him. But she said that her son didn't run with Freddy Clark that much and that he wasn't a gang member or anything like that. She said when they lived in Washington, he ran with a group of boys who called themselves a gang, but they weren't involved in criminal activity to her knowledge.

Rowley asked her questions about activity at 2212 Carpenter - Aunt Zella's house. She mentioned that Freddy Clark and "Jay" did hang out a lot. Then she said that *if* Joe had any money, it was drug money. She wouldn't elaborate on that however. Sharon James named nine additional people that she thought should be interviewed and their names were added to the list of tasks to be performed in the follow-up by detectives.

DECEMBER WAS a cold month in 1992. Late December, with the rapid approach of Christmas, wasn't producing much in the way of evidence to strengthen the case against White and possibly Alf Freddy Clark. People's thoughts were turning to the holidays and local investigators were pretty certain they were going to have to work on Christmas Eve and Christmas Day. Investigators' wives and families were understandably disappointed that the detectives couldn't spend the holidays at home. There were no new leads on the murder weapon and their hopes of Alf Freddy Clark rendering new and valuable information disappeared after the media was tipped off to a new development by "unauthorized police sources." TV reporters announced on December 16th that Alf Freddy Clark was willing to work with investigators to solve the case and to find the gun in return for a "deal". Hearing that on TV, Alf Freddy Clark stopped cooperating immediately in fear of his life. Police investigators were infuriated.

Assistant county attorney Jim Ramey came over to police headquarters and sat down with Lt. Jobe, Sgt. Ervin and Detective Rowley early in December. Ramey told him that he had some bad news - John Wellman, director of the Polk County Adult Defender's Office, was moving to have the Drake Diner case brought to trial quickly. Wellman told the county attorney's office that he was convinced from the beginning by the evidence and information that they had the wrong person. He demanded a speedy trial based on the weight of the existing evidence before this became any more of a media sideshow. Prosecutors were convinced that John Wellman would once again be a formidable adversary in court, particularly in a case with so much importance and publicity. He was a fifty-year-old, successful defense attorney who was highly respected and well known for his victories for indigent clients. John Wellman had been blind since a hunting accident as a teenager.

On Saturday, the 19th, Jo-Jo White attacked a staff member, Tony Rhoads, at Meyer Hall, the juvenile facility where he was being held. Several stitches were required to close the head wound White inflicted on Rhoads. Polk County Youth Services manager Sheila Lumley said the attack was unprovoked. [18] A new charge of assault causing bodily injury was filed against Jo-Jo White. Officials wanted the case moved to adult court and the new charge could now be heard at the hearing. Following this series of developments, John Wellman reinforced his request for rapid adjudication.

The news in December was that president-elect Bill Clinton and his family were spending quiet time at home in Little Rock, Arkansas. Clinton had just finished naming his selections for his incoming cabinet including Mike Espy as agriculture secretary, William Christopher as secretary of state, Lloyd Bentsen for treasury secretary and Madeleine Albright as the new U.N. ambassador. Word was circulating that Mike Ditka was about to be fired as coach of the Chicago Bears. Long lines were expected around Christmas for folks wanting to spend time in a theatre watching "Home Alone 2." The mood in the detective bureau was somber.

BILL BOGGS was working at his desk at headquarters when the detective bureau front desk transferred a call to his phone.

Bill answered, "Detective Boggs."

"Detective, I'm transferring a call to you from King County, Washington P.D. Here it comes."

"This is Detective William Boggs. How can I help you?"

"Boggs, this is Detective John Seltzer with the King County Sheriffs Office, King County, Washington."

"Yes, how ya' doin'?"

Seltzer said, "Good. We've been following up and confirming the whereabouts of the LAR Grizzly .44s in King County here reference your homicide case."

"Yes. All accounted for?"

"All the guns are accounted for – except for one. We have a .44 Grizzly reported stolen here – LAR Grizzly number F000293."

Bill Boggs asked the caller to repeat that, "You have a stolen Grizzly there?" His statement attracted the attention of everyone within earshot in the office.

Seltzer continued, "Stolen from a fella who's a shooter-reloader in Fall City, a few miles outside Kent, Washington here. It was stolen along with some jewelry and other items. Clips for the Grizzly and some ammunition are missing, too. Sold by Fall City Gun Shop in April – stolen in October."

Boggs asked, "Have you talked to this individual?"

"Yep, he's an outdoorsman - sportsman and a reloader. His name is Roger Cline. We have ammunition and expended shell casings from the stolen weapon for comparison that we're sending to you by overnight Fed Ex delivery. You should have this box tomorrow."

Bill thanked Seltzer, got his phone number and said they would stay in touch. Sgt. Ervin walked over and asked Boggs about the phone conversation.

"A stolen Grizzly in Washington State?"

Bill Boggs nodded, "Seattle area."

Ervin shook his head and mumbled, "Come on - be the one. "

Lt. Jobe walked back into the detective office right then, looked around the room, "What's goin' on?"

Boggs stood up and said, "King County, Washington P.D. just called and they have a stolen Grizzly in Seattle – or right outside Seattle."

"You're kidding."

"Nope. It belonged to a guy who was a hunter or something. He reported it stolen a couple of months ago. King County is sending us a package by Fed Ex overnight with ammo from the gun to compare."

Jobe, in his taciturn fashion, said, "Could just be our first stolen or missing one. We've got a lot yet to track down. What else do we know about this one?"

Boggs answered, "Not much - I just now took the call."

Jobe shook his head, "So, how was it stolen? A break-in? Fed Ex'll be here tomorrow?"

"Tomorrow morning."

About 10:00 a.m. the following morning, Fed Ex delivered a large box to the third floor detective office. Rowley, Laddie Jobe, Jim Trotter and most of the crew there in the station that morning watched Bill Boggs slowly open the cardboard box. Trotter marked the items as they were removed from the box. Two 11 ¼ X 15 ½ brown envelopes, marked Envelopes #1 and #2 contained 31 expended shell casings from the stolen .44 and 4 live rounds for the weapon. There was also a preliminary report from the King County, Washington Sheriff's Department indicating some additional possible evidence and a police report on the stolen Grizzly. Jobe looked around and said, "If word of this leaks to the press, gentlemen, I swear I'll find out who did it and they'll hang."

Trotter picked up one of the spent .44 Magnum shell casings from Washington, carefully examined it looking at the extractor marks on the sides of the casing. He turned to Jobe, opening his eyes wide and raising his eyebrows. He said he would personally drive the package and its contents over to the state crime lab.

JOBE ARRIVED at work the next morning so early it was still dark. Bob Ervin appeared at his door while he was still taking his coat off. "Bill McCarthy wants to talk with me and you as soon as he gets in here this morning – before the morning briefing." Jobe didn't even ask him what the reason was. Fifteen minutes later the phone rang and Jobe and Ervin went to the assistant chief's office.

Bill McCarthy was a large man, a veteran investigator, and a man who moved purposefully. His office wall plaques documented many professional achievements including the fact that he was a Marine combat veteran of Vietnam. As they walked in, he slowly laid down a handful of paperwork on his desk, told them to close the door and he sat down slowly in his chair. He told them to sit down. He said, "A stolen Grizzly in Seattle?" Jobe just nodded. "What else do we know?" Ervin and Jobe told him that the Grizzly was apparently stolen from a gun enthusiast outside Seattle and that the theft had been reported to local authorities there. "What next?" McCarthy asked.

Jobe said, "Our people continue tracking down Grizzlys not checked out yet. We're waiting for state lab to get back to us on the ammunition from the Washington hit."

McCarthy nodded, "When's that?"

Jobe replied, "They said they'd push right ahead on this – could be today or tomorrow."

McCarthy looked out the window for a moment and said, "I'm not bringing this up in staff this morning. Let's wait for the state lab report." He turned to Jobe, "Lad, I assume you told your people to keep a tight lid on this. I'm tired of hearing about what we are doing on the news."

Jobe replied, "They have the word – in Technicolor." McCarthy reminded him that Joseph White grew up in the Seattle area. Jobe said, "I'm fully aware of that."

LATER THAT MORNING, Trotter received the results of the state criminalistic lab's examination of the ammunition that came from Washington State. The laboratory analysts said that the submitted, fired .44 Magnum cartridge casings were fired from the same firearm as the two (2) fired Remington .44 Magnum cartridge casings from the Drake Diner. The barrel signature on the jacket of these bullets was consistent with a .44 Magnum auto-loading pistol produced by L.A.R. Manufacturing and marketed as the "Grizzly 44 Mag Mark IV".

Assistant Chief McCarthy was handed the report on the ammunition sent from Washington and he called Jobe and Ervin in to his office. McCarthy scanned them both back-and-forth and said, "What's your plan?" Jobe told him they were still reluctant to send a crew out to Washington at the present time. He felt it was not necessary until they had more information. Bill McCarthy stood up and walked over to the window, thoughtfully looking outside. After a moment he turned to them both and said, "Oh, so you want *their detectives* to run this down at *their* end?" McCarthy paused momentarily and then in an unequivocal voice said, "Nope, get something going on this *now*. Get somebody out there, hook up with their people and get us something!"

Jobe wasn't sure this was the right time to go. He had his own methods and knew he didn't always agree with higher-ups. He often seemed cold to others as a commander but felt it gave him a psychological advantage over his crews and others inside and outside the department. He was sometimes tactless in dealing with subordinates and was surprised if his direction angered and frustrated them, which it often did. When others under his command differed in opinion with him based on their experience, it could get ugly. Add to that the personal acrimony between Jim Rowley and Jobe and people wanted to stay out of their way. Jobe decided under the circumstances to just follow Chief McCarthy's directions.

Jobe went to Detective Boggs and told him to make contact with the officers in Washington and "get the ball rolling." Boggs looked at him waiting for more direction and asked him what the plan was. Jobe said that somebody from the department was going to go out there and find out what's going on. Shortly after that, McCarthy called Jobe back into his office and said that Chief Moulder wanted *action* on this development *now*. Jobe said that since the discovery was in Bill Boggs' area, he should be involved. McCarthy agreed and suggested Jim Rowley, now "head investigator" on the case, should accompany him. That would be the team.

Boggs called John Seltzer back in Seattle and told him they were coming out right after New Years. Seltzer said he thought the trip out there was a good idea. He said, "I'll put our people to work on this. There are some things going on out here that I think might tie into your case. Let me know when you're coming in and we'll see what we can put together. How long do you intend to stay?" Bill Boggs said that depended on how successful they were.

Jim Rowley came home from work that day keyed up as a result of new developments in the case. His wife Connie, sensing something big, watched him rush around and rumble through his closets. She asked him what was going on. Jim stopped, turned to her, and asked her to get his travel bag. She just grinned and asked him where he intended to go. He stopped, took a breath and said, "Bill Boggs and I are going out to Seattle on a stolen Grizzly. Jo-Jo White lived out there. I've got a good feeling about this." Connie couldn't help but smile, looking at Jim's face describing what was happening. She helped him gather clothing and necessities.

Chapter Eight

THE FLIGHT from Des Moines to Seattle was a bumpy one as they proceeded west out of Des Moines. Both detectives were in coach section. The plane wasn't crowded. Jim Rowley sat on the aisle and Bill Boggs had the window with an empty seat in between them. That made it more comfortable since Jim Rowley was a former football lineman who needed his space. Even though there weren't a lot of people onboard there seemed to be a lot of noise and chatter.

Bill Boggs stared out the window deep in thought. Rowley was relaxed, reading a magazine. Boggs turned to him and said, "What is Jobe's problem with this anyway?"

Rowley kept reading his magazine for a moment. He looked up, turned to him and said, "He's always the skeptic. You prove it to me and then we'll let you move ahead if we really need to. You know how he is. What did Seltzer, this detective, say about us coming out?"

"He said it should be an interesting visit."

Rowley laughed and said, "Well, it's gonna be hard for anybody else to take credit for what we did if we come back with case breaking evidence. If we don't, then they'll all back away from this like we've got bubonic plague." On that, Jim continued reading his article about fishing in Canada.

Seattle was chilly. The detectives rented a car, checked into a motel and contacted the King County Sheriff's Department. The deputy on the phone told them how to reach their office.

The next morning when they arrived at the King County facility, they were assigned to work with King County Detective John Seltzer, Badge #127, who worked primarily out of the Fall City Precinct Station. Seltzer, a graying man in his early 50's, was expecting their arrival and greeted them when he appeared at the door.

Rowley introduced himself, "Detective, I'm Jim Rowley from the Des Moines, Iowa PD. This is Detective Bill Boggs who you've talked to."

Seltzer said, "Glad to meet you both". Seltzer smiled at Bill Boggs and said, "We've spoken on the phone quite a bit lately on this. I was the best choice to work with you on this. I'm the one who went out and got the ammunition used in Roger Cline's stolen Grizzly when this whole case began . . ." He hesitated, "Began up here anyway. I packaged it and sent it to you guys. I've talked with Cline already. He wanted to know what was going on but I said we weren't sure and kept a lid on it. He's an interesting individual."

Boggs asked, "Really – how so?"

Seltzer smiled and said, "You'll see. I've got copies of paperwork for you gentlemen." He handed it over to Rowley. One page stood out among the rest: a printout of all guns registered to Roger Frank Cline of 4152 #330 Street Place, SE in Fall City, Washington. Item #2 on the list was a .44 LAR Grizzly, serial number F000293, purchased April 15th, 1992 from Dealer 09036, Fall City Gun Shop.

Rowley asked Detective Seltzer, "What are the chances we could go out and talk with Roger Cline today?" Seltzer said the chances were excellent. He had already made arrangements to drive out to see him. Seltzer said he heard the stolen Grizzly had not been recovered. Both detectives answered that it was not. Seltzer knew enough to leave that subject alone for now.

It was still early in the morning when the detectives joined Seltzer in a King County unmarked car and headed east. The King County scenery was picturesque with the hilly ruggedness that characterized the Northwest Territory in older times. They stopped for coffee at Rose's Bake Shop. It was full of early morning customers who came by for their pastries. Detective Seltzer quietly asked Jim Rowley for details of this crime in Des Moines: Jim responded and talked briefly about the crime itself: the viciousness; the extreme pressure on the department to solve it; details of the head wounds to the victims; the devastated families of the victims and Jo-Jo White, formerly from their area - the suspect. Seltzer seemed intrigued by Rowley's short to-the-point account. He took a moment, glanced out at their parked car outside, turned back and said they should probably go see Roger Cline without delay.

ROGER CLINE'S home was outside of town. The area was not well developed which was a departure from some of the Seattle and King County areas that they had seen. They pulled up to a modest but nice residence with a garage and out building and got out of the car. The officers were greeted by Cline when they approached the front door. Seltzer was right – this man was big, a hulk of a man weighing more than 300 pounds. He had the bearded, rugged looking weathered skin of an outdoorsman. He was a hunter, his looks reminiscent of hunters of this area in days long gone. His temperament appeared serious, no-nonsense.

Seltzer introduced the Des Moines officers, who showed Cline their IDs. Cline invited them inside. Seltzer said, "Mr. Cline, tell us about the Grizzly you owned and what exactly happened."

Cline said, "I bought the gun on April 15th from Fall City Gun Shop and it was here for sure until October 8th. I discovered it missing on October 15th. I searched the house and cabin and it was gone along with three clips of my hand-loaded ammunition. Some of my wife's jewelry is gone, too. So I went ahead and reported it all to the police." Boggs mentioned that he had already seen the original police report.

Bill Boggs asked him, "Mr. Cline, these LAR Grizzlys are pretty rare - they are very powerful weapons. How is it that you bought one? I mean, what did you plan to use it for?"

"I pan for gold and I spend a lot of time out roughing it. The 'Griz,' that gun, is good protection against bears. It'll stop them cold."

Jim Rowley asked him, "Where do you store your guns? Are they locked up?"

"Yes, I have a lot of guns and I'm careful about that. I'm a hand loader. All my supplies and equipment are kept safe."

"Does anyone else have access to these guns?" Cline answered no.

Rowley asked him, "Mr. Cline, I'm sure the investigating officers asked you this already, but do you have any idea who might have taken this gun? I understand there were no signs of a forcible entry – no signs of a break-in."

Roger Cline shook his head and answered, "I don't have a clue on that."

Rowley continued, "How many people know that you owned a Grizzly?"

Cline thought for a minute and said, "Probably fifteen people tops."

"Of those fifteen people, do any of them come to mind at all?"

"No sir, none whatsoever. I don't make a habit of associating with anyone who I think would do something like this." An angry expression settled over Cline's face and he added, "And if I found out it was someone I knew did this, I'd kill 'em!" The officers thanked him for his cooperation and assured him that they would contact him if any additional information on his missing Grizzly came up. Their next stop was The Fall City Gun Shop. The owner of the Fall City Gun Shop, Greg Howard, confirmed that Roger Cline did have a large collection of firearms, was an avid shooter and was a good customer. The officers asked him if Cline filled out the

ATF paperwork for the purchase of the Grizzly. Howard found it and showed it to them.

Bill Boggs asked Seltzer what their next stop would be. He said they were going over to 712 Walnut in Kent, the Springwood Housing Project. Seltzer said, "We're gonna meet Mitzi Johanakencth over there. She's the King County Sheriff's Officer at the Project. I found out that White ran with two guys there where he lived – a Bill Howe and a Kendal Van Ward. The officers went to the apartments where one lived and one hung out but found no one. They asked around but nobody was forthcoming with any information. Nobody wanted to cooperate. They left police business cards requesting a callback but didn't expect to hear anything."

Seltzer, Rowley and Boggs paid a visit to the police station at Kent, Washington. They were introduced to Detective Sergeant R.M. Holt. He said to Rowley and Boggs, "Gentlemen, I've got something that ties into your case. I've got an incident report and the trip sheet on something that happened over at the Springwood Housing Project. The manager over there, Terry Brew, called 911 and reported hearing a series of very loud gunshots that came from apartment D105. You know who lived there? Joseph White and his mother. One of our officers, Rusty Walker, responded to the call. I've talked to him. He went through the apartment. Joe White was there, uncooperative when questioned. Anyway, Walker found an expended brass .44 magnum shell casing and a large leather shoulder holster harness set-up with a spare .44 clip in it. Walker confiscated them. Plus, he found more .44 shell casings on the apartment roof, in the rain gutter up there."

Rowley asked, "Where are the confiscated items – the shoulder holster, clip and rounds?" Sgt. Holt said that the actual shoulder holster itself was *not* found, just the harness, clip and the shell casings. He said they were checked in at the police property area. Rowley said, "We'd like to take them out to show to the owner of the stolen Grizzly, this Mr. Cline." Holt said he would arrange for release of the materials. The detectives thanked him for his help.

Bill Boggs said they would like to talk with Officer Walker if possible. Holt said that he would get him to come to the station and meet with them. They asked Sergeant Holt about the two boys Seltzer said were associates of Whites. Holt said that Bill Howe didn't ring a bell, but that Kendall Van Ward had been stopped several times with Joseph White when he still lived up there.

Later that day, around 6 p.m., Boggs and Rowley stopped in at a barbeque joint that Seltzer had suggested called Cubby's Rib House. They were sitting and talking about the developments of the day. Boggs said, "That Roger Cline? He's a big one, ain't he?"

Rowley wiped the barbecue sauce off his chin and said, "He's definitely a no bullshit individual. If White had tried to steal this guy's gun from him, these cops would be investigating a homicide with Jo-Jo with a wound hole the size of a grapefruit to show for it. I suppose White could have been involved in a break-in at Cline's, but that doesn't make much sense either – out there in the sticks and all. Plus, Cline has dogs." Bill Boggs asked him if he was planning to call in with details of their trip. Jim Rowley laid his half finished rib down, wiped his hands off, took a slow draw off his drink, wiped his hands off again and said, "Nope." Bill Boggs looked at him but didn't even bother to ask why not.

ON THEIR SECOND DAY in Seattle, Rowley, Boggs and John Seltzer made another trip out to the Roger Cline residence to talk with him. When they arrived and were seated, Seltzer removed the tan colored leather shoulder harness from a black evidence bag and Cline's attention was immediately drawn to it. They asked him, in some very obvious anticipation, to try it on. Cline stood up and tried on the harness. It fit him perfectly. He gave the officers an ironclad stare and said, "This is mine!"

The harness had a spare, empty .44 clip in it. He said the harness was definitely the one that he bought for $25 at a gun show in Puyallup, Washington. The spare clip looked exactly like the one he bought at the same gun show for $60. Roger Cline then became expressionless. He slowly leaned over and purposefully asked, "Where did you find these?" The detectives sat silent. Roger Cline scanned their expressions, shook his head and rephrased his question, "God damn it, where did you find these?"

Detective Seltzer hesitated for a moment and answered, "They came from an apartment at the Springwood Housing Project. The woman who lives there is Sharon James. She's a black woman about thirty-five years old. Her son, Joseph White, lives there, too. Does either name ring a bell with you?"

Roger Cline stared at Seltzer and Rowley and said, "She's black?"

Seltzer acknowledged, "Yes, she's black."

Cline exhaled loudly, "No - absolutely not. That wouldn't be anybody we would know. So, where's my gun?"

Jim Rowley nodded and said, "We're working on that."

Cline lunged forward in his seat, stared at Rowley with a chilling stare and said, "So after all of this, you haven't recovered my fucking gun?"

Rowley looked at him and said, "No, we have not." Again, they told Cline they would be following up with him with any new information. Cline said he wanted answers.

The detectives got in their car to leave and Rowley said, "Did anyone else notice the vein pop out in this man's forehead? He was ready to go at the drop of a hat. Here's a guy with a serious temper – I pity the bears."

The detectives thought that if Jo-Jo White was in possession of Cline's .44 Magnum in the Seattle area, there was a good chance that he might have been involved in robberies and other crime - using or displaying this powerful weapon. Later on that day, Rowley and Seltzer went to the King County Sheriff's Department Homicide and Major Offense Bureau only to find that this department had no unsolved crimes involving a .44 magnum automatic. Bureau Officer Ray Fisher said, "A .44 Magnum automatic would be rare and an awfully big weapon to be used in a robbery/homicide." Rowley concurred.

Seltzer and Rowley stopped by Kent High School in a community with a coincidental sounding name - South Des Moines, Washington. They met with Mark Weston, the principal, and Gina Raban, head of security. The officers showed them their identification and without any prompting on their part, Mark Weston said they were probably there concerning Joseph White. Gina Raban said Joseph White was trouble and both of them stated he was a gang member in the Bloods. However, they didn't recall any problems involving a gun and White. He was actually expelled for truancy. They said the school had done some in-home work with him but that didn't work out due to the home environment and the people hanging around there.

Principal Weston did some checking with the Seattle School System for the detectives while they were there. They obtained a six-page fax from Denny Middle School in Seattle stating that Joseph White was expelled for having a revolver. Weston also indicated that someone from the State of Iowa had earlier asked for and been sent all of Joseph Hodges White's records. Rowley wasn't surprised since Iowa DCI agent Doug Fagan had been working the case for the state from Des Moines.

The detectives returned to the Kent Police Department to interview the officer who responded to the report of gunshots at the housing complex. Jim Rowley interviewed Rusty Walker, Badge #0152, a seven-year officer who worked bike patrol with Officer Roy Wilcowski.

Officer Walker said, "We were responding to a call from Terry Brew, the apartment manager, reference shots fired. When we got there, we were met by the Brews who had been standing in front of the building where Sharon James, Joseph White and some other family members lived. They heard several rounds going off and a round, or shell casing, hitting the gutters and tinkling around in there. We figured if White had a gun, we wanted to get it. The Brews said it sounded like an auto loader by the way it was spitting shells out."

"So we went to the apartment and were allowed in. There was a black male juvenile there. We asked him his name and he gave us what we believed to be a fake name. Joseph White was there in the apartment, too. We have had plenty of problems with him. We asked him about the gun and he came on with his normal attitude, stating he 'knew nuttin' 'bout no gun'. Then the mother, Sharon James, arrived and reluctantly gave us permission to search the apartment. You could access the roof right out of White's bedroom window. I went up on the roof of the complex and in the gutter I found one spent .44 shell. So I went back down to White's bedroom and found the shoulder holster rig with a clip in it and one spent shell on the floor. The Brews told me earlier that they walked out a short distance from the building to get a look at the roof area and they saw that shoulder holster lying up there. Of course, it was gone when we arrived."

"I asked White about these items and he said it wasn't illegal to have that stuff and he denied having the gun. I made out a juvenile appearance card and made an appointment for him to come in. I confiscated the items and brought them in and secured them as property." Sgt. Holt turned these items over to Detective Rowley to take with him back to Des Moines as evidence.

Following the interview with Officer Walker, Rowley, Boggs and members of the King County Sheriff's Office went to 702 West Waterman to interview three people who heard a series of five loud explosions that they thought were M80s. These people walked outside to see where the explosions came from. They heard a sixth shot and pinpointed the sound definitely coming from the roof of White's building.

EARLY ON THE MORNING of January 6th, the Des Moines detectives met with Detectives Seltzer and C.K. Webster of

King County. Seltzer knew that some groups of local kids ran together, blacks and whites, and had been involved in some thefts, house-prowls, drugs and trouble. Police felt that this group possibly held the key to figuring out how Joseph White came into possession of Cline's LAR Grizzly.

Seltzer knew of a girl, Kimberly Anders, who ran with these kids. She lived in Fall City and might be able to help them out on this. All four officers decided to pay a visit to the Anders' residence at 32712 SE 43rd in Fall City. Kimberly Louise Anders was home. She was a junior at Two Rivers High School. She talked with Seltzer about her friends and what she did - besides go to school. Seltzer asked her if she knew the name Joseph White. She hesitated, but said that she knew the guy they were probably asking about who she only knew as "Joe". Seltzer described him and Kim reluctantly acknowledged that it was him.

Seltzer asked her, "Does Joe know Johanna Cline, Roger Cline's daughter?"

She sat silent for a moment and then nodded and answered, "Yes, I was there when they were introduced to each other."

The detectives calmly but carefully exchanged glances with each other. Kim Anders was extremely nervous and said she did not want to be involved. Seltzer raised his voice and told her to come clean or they would take her downtown for further questioning. She said, shaking and in tears, that Joe White and Johanna dated for about two months. Kimberly reluctantly went on to say that Joe White had been in the Cline home many times while the parents were out of town at their cabin. The parents would leave and then she, Joe White, Johanna and Marlin Curry would party at Cline's home. Asked about Marlin Curry, Kim said that Marlin Curry was a friend of hers from Kent who actually introduced her to Joe White. When asked to describe Marlin Curry, she described him as black, young, tall, thin with a scar. The officers thought that Marlin Curry's description fit the juvenile who gave them a fake name when the Kent PD were investigating the gunshots at the Springwood Housing Project. Conclusions following interviews with local kids who ran with Johanna were that, according to them, Johanna and Jo-Jo White were lovers.

She said that the reason Johanna Cline hadn't shed some light on who stole her dad's property was not only because she was told not to have people in the home while the parents were gone – it was because her father, Roger Cline, was extremely prejudiced against blacks. If he ever found out that his daughter, Johanna, had a black boy in their home in Fall City it would be terrible.

Rowley taped a formal interview that coincided closely with what she said in the impromptu session. In addition, he asked her if Johanna said anything to her about Joe White and the burglary. She said no. He asked if she had ever been to Joe White's house. She said no. He asked her if she had ever seen Joe White with a firearm in the past. She said yes, but it was a small revolver.

Following the Kimberly Anders interview, the detectives returned to the Fall City Police Substation. John Seltzer knew what the next step would be. He made some phone calls. Johanna Cline was at Mount Si High School in Snoqualmie.

All four detectives drove to Mount Si High School. They walked into the school and were directed to the Office of the Principal, Dave Humphries. They identified themselves, and told him the nature of their visit. He had Johanna Cline summoned to the office. John Seltzer said he wanted to interview her alone to set the stage for Rowley and Boggs.

Seltzer had her come in to a private room and sit down. Seltzer, an expert interrogator with a usually intimidating voice, adopted a quieter, more disarming tone for Johanna Cline. He smiled, identified himself and asked her, "Do you know a Joseph White?"

Johanna gave him an annoyed look and said, "No."

"Now, Johanna, we have information that you do know him."

After a moment, she replied, "Okay, but I only knew him as Joe."

Seltzer slowly continued, "Have you ever had Joe in your family home?"

"No."

"Again, Johanna, we hear from reputable sources that you have had him in the home. Now, do you want to think for a minute about that?"

"Okay, I did have him there at different times."

"And when was that? Do you remember? I've got a calendar right here." She looked at the calendar.

"I think the night when he spent the night was October 10th."

"Was anyone else there that night?"

"Yes, another girl and a guy, Marlin Curry."

"Did you see anyone go near the area where your father keeps his guns stored?"

"No. The gun room is always locked."

John Seltzer looked closely at Johanna and said, "Johanna, something happened. Your father's gun was fired at Joe White's residence in Kent. The shells were recovered and identified as being fired from your dad's gun. Your dad's holster was recovered from White's apartment. Now, either Joe White took the gun, or was present when it was taken, or it was given to him."

"I didn't give it to him!"

"But don't you agree that one of those events had to take place for him to have the gun?"

Johanna conceded, "I guess that's what it looks like." She went on to say that her parents knew nothing of her dating, hanging with or running with blacks. She said her father would go crazy.

THE DETECTIVES were obliged to pay a repeat visit to Roger Cline and apprise him of their findings in regard to his weapon, but more important, the part his daughter had played in what happened. They had no choice in the matter. They arrived at Cline's home, got out of the unmarked car and went to the door. Roger Cline met them at the door and invited them in. John Seltzer and Rowley asked Roger Cline to listen carefully and Seltzer explained the Washington State Domestic Abuse Code to him. Roger Cline asked what that had to do with him.

They explained to him that his .44 Grizzly had been taken to Des Moines, Iowa and used in the double homicide at the Drake Diner. Cline immediately looked upset and he asked how this could have occurred – what chain of events could have ended like that? They continued that his daughter, Johanna, against his wishes, had parties at their house while they were away. Roger Cline became infuriated hearing this news. Then he stopped suddenly. He asked who took his gun. Rowley told him that it was a seventeen-year-old black teenager named Joseph Hodges White who was originally from Des Moines, but who had grown up in the Seattle area and had been in their home. Roger Cline screamed, "My daughter had a fuckin' nigger in my house?" He broke his TV remote in half in a rage.

Rowley told him to sit down and listen. Rowley pointed his index finger in Cline's face and said, "That is the last time I want to hear that word come out of your mouth! You and your daughter are going to Des Moines and you're going to be my star witnesses in his trial! Do you understand?" Roger Cline was now bawling and said he would do whatever was necessary to put the killer behind bars.

Following the interview with Roger Cline, the officers returned to the Fall City station. Pulling the case together was creating a great deal of satisfaction, not only for the Des Moines detectives, but also for the Washington officers who were proud of their accomplishment and "good street police work" on the case. Boggs and Rowley were given several mementos of the trip including King County police badges. King County's officers said they would continue to look for evidence in the case and said their personnel would be available if summoned to come to Des Moines to testify. John Seltzer wished them a good trip home and all the luck to get the conviction they were looking for.

Boggs and Rowley flew home late on Sunday and went home exhausted from a weekend of events that would stay with them for a long time. Jim Rowley pulled in his driveway and was met at the door by his wife Connie. She asked him if the trip was what they wanted. Jim said it was, went in, unloaded his bags and said he was exhausted. Jim knew that Monday morning at the station would be intense. Connie said there was a message for him that they had a meeting first thing Monday with Jobe and the county attorneys.

THE DETECTIVES all rode over to the meeting with the county attorneys in one car. Lt. Jobe said, "You could have called us for an update while this was going on out there. You know we wanted to know what the hell was going on." Rowley said that the situation was developing hour-by-hour and that changes in the situation would have made a bunch of calls unnecessary. Jobe disagreed.

They went into the county attorney's office and were shown to the conference room where they took seats and waited. They were joined by Polk County Attorney John Sarcone and Assistant County Attorney Jim Ramey. Ramey carefully laid down his stacks of files on the table, sat down, took a deep breath, looked at Jim Rowley and said, "Well?"

Jim Rowley looked around the room and said, "The Cline daughter took Jo-Jo White out to the parent's house and screwed him while they were away on the weekends and he stole the Grizzly – end of story." Ramey threw his pen down on the table and asked politely for a few more details. Rowley calmly asked Ramey which particular part he needed more details on and everybody laughed. Rowley continued, "These officers out there were great. There were a bunch of kids breaking into residences, looking for money, drugs, whatever and the Cline girl was running with them and the King County cops knew about it and tracked them down. Plus, White fired the stolen weapon back at his crib, up on the roof – cops got a call on that and confiscated fired casings from the Grizzly along with a part of the shoulder harness stolen from Roger Cline. He has positively identified the harness as one he bought at a gun show out there."

John Sarcone asked, "Did you talk to the officers that investigated the rooftop firing?"

"Yes, sir."

"And are they willing to come and testify to that effect?"

"Yes, sir."

Sarcone continued, "What about Cline and his daughter. What kind of witnesses are they going to be?"

Rowley took a deep breath, looked over at Bill Boggs and said, "He wants the son-of-a-bitch hung. The daughter, Johanna, folded the minute she was busted on this deal. Cline said he wanted to kill her. He was serious. This man seems to be white supremacist material. He found out that his gun killed two white people in Des Moines and he went berserk!" Sarcone looked at Bill Boggs and asked if that was true. Boggs said it was, adding that Cline looked like he lost his mind momentarily until they settled him down. He said the Cline girl couldn't have committed a worse sin in the eyes of her father. Boggs added that Cline started bawling out loud about the Drake Diner victims and their families.

Ramey was writing on a yellow legal pad, stopped, looked up and asked what else. Rowley leaned back in his chair, looked at the ceiling, looked at Ramey and continued. "Cline's daughter's best friend is the one who tied this all together. She told us that Joe White and Johanna Cline had been dating all along. She had been out at the love shack with them and a friend of White's, one Marlin Curry, it's in my notes. They partied out at the parents' house. Parents were gone on the weekends and the whole thing is in our notes. The girls are lying, to make the parties at the house sound milder than we're all thinking they were. The officers from the rooftop gunshot incident in town questioned Jo-Jo's mother, Sharon James, and she gave them permission to search the apartment. We've got a good search there. We've talked to school officials and they gave us a picture of a troubled, disruptive, ganged-up little asshole who they tried to help but who "spit the bit" - guns involved, charges filed etcetera, etcetera."

Ramey continued writing, then stopped, looked over at John Sarcone and said, "John Wellman will not be pleased when he hears this. There goes his goddamn case. And tomorrow, we're getting the case moved to adult court." Sarcone said he would make the call to Wellman himself and set up a meeting to discuss these developments. He congratulated Rowley and Boggs for doing a terrific job out in Washington pulling this together. Jobe said that even though the police knew early on that White had lived in Seattle, nobody put it together and thought it would roll out like this. Jim Rowley wondered to himself why Jobe, as unit commander, did not make it easier for them to proceed when they had a match on Roger Cline's Grizzly. Ramey added that of all the cases they had prosecuted against John Wellman, this one was going to be one for the books.

Chapter Nine

THE COURT RULED in favor of the county attorney's petition
and moved Joseph Hodges White's trial to adult court. Following
that expected ruling, arrangements were made to sit down with
attorney John Wellman and discuss the new evidence that had
surfaced as a result of the Washington trip. At that meeting,
John Wellman acted as if it didn't make as much difference as
the county attorney's asserted. He questioned the value of the
evidence and still said that they had the wrong boy. Jim Ramey
said, "We're prepared to bring all of these people in – all of them,
and put 'em on the stand." John Wellman was silent. Following
that meeting, little more was heard from Wellman about
moving to a speedy trial. That same day, Alf Freddy Clark
was moved from the juvenile detention center in Chariton to
the Meyer Hall juvenile facility in Des Moines to await an
upcoming parole violation hearing.

IN SPITE of the orders from police senior commanders
to avoid any discussion of developments in the murder
investigation, reporters began asking specific questions during
briefings indicating that somebody with the police department
was talking "out of school." It was frustrating to both the Des
Moines Police Department and to the Polk County Attorneys
Office who were trying to keep critical evidence relating to the
case confidential. Mishandled evidence could jeopardize the
entire case. Nobody even wanted to think about the victims'

families, the public and the media's reactions in this high profile case if White walked because of mishandled evidence. Assistant Chief McCarthy concluded after meeting with Chief Moulder and County Attorney John Sarcone that they needed a press conference to quell rumors and evidence leaks.

The police department held a press conference to clear the air on the investigation. McCarthy and Jobe told the members of the press that they would give them anything they could to bring them up to date on the progress in the Drake Diner investigation. Immediately, reporters asked about new evidence that had been obtained in recent days and the significance of it to the investigation. The obvious leak of sensitive information annoyed Jobe. He looked at the inquiring reporter and said that the department would not discuss it or its value *at this time*. He said that the investigation was winding down this week and that the extra officers assigned to the case would be reporting for regular duty on Thursday.

One of the local TV anchors asked Bill McCarthy, "Chief, did you find the gun? Is that the new evidence?"

McCarthy stood there thinking for a moment and answered, "We still don't have the gun, and there's still a substantial amount of money available to the person who can produce it." The anchor asked how much money and McCarthy replied $10,000. Another reporter asked McCarthy about Alf Freddy Clark and what his status currently was. Again, McCarthy stood quietly for a moment then said, "Clark probably will be charged in the crime but whether it is murder or some other crime remains under study. The county attorney will decide that."

A reporter asked if the police department was "keeping the county attorney's office in *the loop*" on the progress of the investigation or not. McCarthy quickly answered, "By the end of the week, the county attorney will probably have everything we have. We're at a point where every written document will be examined and some judgment will be made."

Pressing the point on the newly discovered evidence in the case, another reporter asked why officers had been sent to Seattle concerning the Drake Diner case. Jobe answered matter-of-factly, "To do background checks on White." Taking no further questions, they thanked the reporters for the cooperation and the press briefing was closed.

IN THE WEEKS that followed, Joseph White and Alf Freddy Clark remained in jail. Public defender John Wellman and his team were preparing to defend White. Jim Ramey, Steve Foritano and the staff of the Polk County Attorney's Office were assembling a case against White to present to the court. In a meeting, Foritano reviewed the bloody crime scene photos from the diner and wondered if psychological counseling should be offered to jurors after they review the graphic photo displays – the photos were that intense. Des Moines Police continued to interview witnesses and the hunt for the murder weapon was still on.

Standard procedure at the Polk County Jail was to conduct cell searches for contraband on an unannounced basis. It was called a "shake-out." According to Jeff Cronin, a Des Moines policeman who was working in the Polk County Jail at the time, Joseph White was a prisoner prone to fighting and assaults on other inmates. In March, an unannounced cell "shakedown" discovered drawings made by Joseph White in his cell. They illustrated a black gang member in gang colors with an automatic pistol pointed at the heads of white victims and shooting them. The drawings were confiscated and taken to the Polk County Attorney's Office. They became evidence in the case.

Early in April, a twenty-one year old restaurant manager in Phoenix was shot to death because he wouldn't open the safe for three armed robbers. Lyle Burnett heard about the murder and wrote a letter to the parents of the dead boy. He said, "You don't know me but I know how it feels."

John Wellman requested a change in venue from Judge Ray
Fenton. He claimed that the publicity surrounding the case made
a fair trial impossible in Polk County. Under supervision of the
court, a questionnaire was submitted to a jury panel to see if
they felt White could receive a fair trial in Polk County. Results
of the questionnaire were analyzed and Judge Fenton ruled
that he felt a fair trial was possible without a change in venue.
The judge said that saturation media coverage of the crime had
been limited to the first few days following the crime. He also
said that the coverage did not focus on Joseph White. During
a pre-trial evidence suppression hearing, Wellman tried to
suppress Johanna Cline's statements she made to the detectives
in Washington State. He claimed Ms. Cline was not aware of
her rights at the time. The county attorneys advised him that
the State of Washington has no law on the books regarding the
rights of a juvenile during questioning and interrogation.

Prior to the beginning of the trial, John Wellman met with
members of Joseph White's family. He expressed his belief to
them that Joseph was innocent of the crime and told them that
he was going to do everything possible to prove that police had a
flimsy case and the wrong person charged with the robbery and
murders. Wellman's reputation in tough cases was a source of
strength for the family.

Wellman's opponent in the case would be prosecutor
James William Ramey. Working on behalf of the Polk County
Attorney's Office he won forty-five murder convictions in ten
years. He earned his law degree in 1975 and went to work for
the Polk County Attorney's Office, under the leadership of
Dan Johnston. People in the office remembered him as an
excellent prosecutor. One assistant added that he could be
arrogant, had a temper and lacked people skills with people in
that office. Jim Ramey even said, "My mouth is always getting
me in trouble . . . I guess I'm too callous and too blunt."

After his original stint with Polk County, Jim Ramey went
into private practice for awhile, then becoming a member of Iowa

Attorney General Tom Miller's team in 1981. He successfully prosecuted a man accused of murdering a Newton, Iowa police officer and won several other high profile cases. Many people criticized his bravado style, but his success in the courtroom was becoming legendary. He angered people, crossed the line, got convictions and made headlines. Defense counsels hated him. Des Moines police officers commented that Jim Ramey was "hell in the courtroom." But they also said that his behavior and comments outside the courtroom subjected him to a lot of heat. In 1991, John Sarcone was elected Polk County Attorney. John said he quickly rehired Ramey and put him in charge of the Polk County major-offense bureau.

Chapter Ten

JURY SELECTION was conducted on Monday, May 3rd and Tuesday, May 4th. Lawyers questioned 20 potential jurors on Monday and on Tuesday conducted individual and group questioning sessions. The jury of 11 whites and one black was impaneled for the trial to begin the following morning.

The courtroom was packed as the trial began Wednesday morning. Witnesses, families, reporters, TV cameras and crews left little space. One long oak table would serve both prosecution and defense. Prior to the proceedings, prosecutor James Ramey and assistant prosecutor Steve Foritano were seated at the table reviewing notes. John Wellman and his legal assistant were at the other end of the table talking as five sheriff's deputies brought Joseph White into the courtroom. White was wearing a dark blue suit, white shirt, his hair neatly cut. He looked around at his relatives and supporters and smiled.

After everyone was seated, the court attendant told everyone to rise as Judge Ray Fenton entered the courtroom and stepped up to his bench. He addressed the jury, telling them that the charges against Mr. White were two counts of first-degree murder and one count of first-degree robbery. He addressed those in the courtroom emphasizing the importance of a fair proceeding and warned that the proceedings would be conducted in an orderly manner. He warned that outbursts, threatening behaviors and disruptions would not be tolerated.

Ramey and Foritano's opening statement to the jury focused on their intent to prove beyond a reasonable doubt that Joseph Hodges White, Jr. was the lone gunman, killer and robber that night, November 29th, 1992, at the Drake Diner that took the lives of Cara McGrane and Harry Timothy Burnett. Ramey told the court that Joseph White, Jr. stole the gun near Seattle, brought it to Des Moines in November, 1992, and fired it in Des Moines on three separate occasions. He said that forensic evidence presented would link White and the gun to the murders at the diner. Steve Foritano said that eyewitnesses would testify that White was the gunman and witnesses would also testify that he threw a party at a local hotel after the crime using money stolen from the Drake Diner.

John Wellman's opening defense statement was that Joe White did, in fact, bring the handgun to Des Moines but he couldn't have used it at the Drake Diner because witnesses in his home would place Joe White waking up from a nap shortly after the crime was committed. Further, he said that witnesses for the prosecution had conflicting stories and conflicting accounts of the gunman's description that did not match Mr. White.

After a short recess, the first prosecution witness, Dontrell Ducker, was summoned to the witness stand and sworn in. Ducker related that he was working that night at the diner, witnessed the shooting, saw the gunman and noticed the gap in his front teeth. Jim Ramey asked him, "Would it help if you could see the gap in his teeth?"

"Yes."

White was ordered to stand and expose his front teeth to the witness.

Ramey said, "Dontrell, is there any question that's the man you saw?"

Ducker answered, "No."

Wellman asked Ducker on cross-examination, "Mr. Ducker, are you positive Joseph White has a gap in his teeth?"

"Yes."

Wellman reminded him that he told police he thought *maybe* he had a gap in his teeth. He then asked if Ducker had known White prior to the crime. Ducker said that he had. Wellman asked if that in some way might have clouded his judgment.

Ducker said, "I knew him a long time ago. I found it hard to believe that he would do it, but I'm sure he's the person I saw."

Following cross-examination, Ramey asked Dontrell Ducker if he was sure the person he saw wasn't Alf Freddy Clark. Ducker said it was not. Ducker was thanked for his cooperation and dismissed.

Eleven-year-old Maggie O'Brien was called to the stand. She testified that she was with her family that night – her brother Tom, thirteen, and her sister Molly who was fifteen – and they were sitting close to where the incident occurred. Her brother and sister said that they couldn't positively identify the shooter. Maggie said she heard the first shot and dove and hid under the table. Following Ramey's question as to the identity of the shooter, she confirmed White was the shooter that night at the diner.

On cross-examination, John Wellman asked her if she was absolutely positive White was the man she saw. She gave a puzzled look and said, "I don't feel he is the person but he looks very much like the person I saw." Following that, Jim Ramey asked her again if White was the person she saw and she said that he was. After she was excused from the witness stand, she sat in her mother's lap and cried.

Lisa Taylor was called to the witness stand following Maggie O'Brien. She testified that she was working as a waitress that night and that she got a side view of the gunman. She said, "I was walking by and looked at him and looked at Cara and when I looked back I could tell something was wrong – that the man was robbing the restaurant. At that time, he shot Cara and the last thing I remember is seeing Tim running toward the cash register." Under cross-examination she admitted telling police that she did not see the gunman's face and that she didn't think she could identify him.

The final witness of the opening court session was Mary Burnett, Tim's wife. During very emotional testimony, she related that they were at the diner decorating the Christmas tree that night. She said at the sound of the first shot, Tim pushed her outside onto the patio and told her to stay down until he came back. She was in tears giving her testimony. She looked toward the courtroom ceiling trying unsuccessfully to keep from crying and said, "I heard another bang. I got up and a waitress came and said 'It's Tim and it's very bad, very bad'. I was screaming 'No' and I remember running halfway down the bar and someone stopped me from there." She was excused from the witness stand to regain her composure. Several spectators were openly crying during and following her testimony as well.

Des Moines' NBC affiliate WHO-TV 13 arranged and carried live coverage of the trial on Cable Channel 12, which was usually the Home Shopping Network. It was a C-SPAN type feed using no analysis or comment. WHO worked together with TCI Cablevision to make it available to cable subscribers. People who did not have cable were angry about the medium selected to broadcast the trial. The CBS affiliate KCCI-TV8 approached TCI first, but TCI spokesman Rich Gilman said that TCI was already set up with WHO on other projects. KCCI-TV's news director Dave Busiek announced more accessible coverage through a TV8 nightly half hour special following the 10:00 p.m. news each night during the trial.

THE TRIAL continued Thursday, May 6th with more witnesses for the prosecution. One of the prosecution's most damaging witnesses was Scott Birrer. He was a third year Drake law student who had dated Cara McGrane in the past. Birrer testified that he was facing Cara talking to her about the Thanksgiving vacation that was ending. He said the killer appeared behind her in the cash register area and put his hand on her shoulder. He said she turned and looked at the man, asked him what he wanted and turned back to him (Birrer). Birrer said, "We were looking eye-to-eye when the gun appeared in his hand. My thought was that he was just going to rob, and wouldn't shoot. Right as I was thinking the word 'shoot' he fired and Cara jerked and quickly fell."

Birrer said he dropped to the floor and was back on his knees when he saw Tim Burnett running toward the cash register. He said as Tim Burnett went out of his line of sight, he heard a second shot. Ramey said, "The person you saw shoot Cara McGrane, did you get a good enough look at him to be able to identify him?"

"Yes."

"Is he in the courtroom?"

"Yes, it's the individual sitting right there," pointing toward White.

Ramey said, "Let the record show he's identified Joseph Hodges White."

On cross-examination of Scott Birrer, Wellman said, "Mr. Birrer, Cara was a good friend of yours, and you really want to participate in solving this case and identifying Mr. White – correct?"

Birrer replied, "I've spent three years of my life studying the law. I would never use the law or use what I have to say to meet my own goals – there's no hidden agenda."

Former waitress Janet Pittman testified she was standing near the jukebox and heard a loud noise. She saw a man with a wild look on his face holding a gun. She described him as 5' 7" to 5' 10" – 170 lbs. She said he had a gap in his teeth. Assistant prosecutor Steve Foritano asked her if she got a good enough look at him to be able to identify him. She said she could if she could see his teeth. Again, White was told to stand and expose his front teeth. She looked at him momentarily, looked away and said, "Yes, that's him."

Wellman countered that Pittman told the police that she didn't think she could identify the assailant and that she didn't mention the gap in his teeth to police either. She answered that her memory had been triggered when she saw White's mother, Sharon James, on TV and she saw the gap in her front teeth. She said she gave the information to the county attorney's office two or three weeks ago.

Wellman said, "You couldn't identify my client from looking at his face, only after looking at his teeth?"

She answered, "That's what makes me sure."

Deputy State Medical Examiner Francis Garrity, who performed the autopsies, testified, "Both died instantly from gunshot wounds to the head. In McGrane's case, the gun was held to her right cheek and fired. Burnett was shot from a distance of at least two to three feet." The damage to both victims' heads had been so severe that Dr. Garrity had to stitch areas of them back together during the autopsies to establish the locations of the entrance and exit wounds.

Detectives continued their daily tasks of investigation, case supplementaries and court testimony on other cases during the trial – the daily workload continued. On Thursday, Jobe had a written death threat to hand to Jim Rowley – anonymous, of course. Jim laughed, wadded it up and threw it in the garbage.

On Friday, the audiotapes of the interrogation of Joseph White on the night of his arrest were played. Everyone in the courtroom, particularly the jury, listened intently. Following that, Jim Ramey asked Sgt. Ralph Roth on the stand, one of the two initial interrogators, why Jo-Jo White would have made the comment on the tapes that he thought about coming forward to police to help out with information. After all, White had denied knowing anything about the gun or the murders. Roth said Joseph White couldn't explain that. John Wellman shook his head impatiently and questioned the accuracy of the interview tapes. He claimed *one word* had been changed in a second transcript of the tapes his office had received. Jim Ramey objected vigorously to the bench, "Mr. Wellman is grand-standing for the TV and the spectators."

The prosecution produced a large envelope that contained police photographs of the crime scene at the Drake Diner and asked that it be entered as evidence. Ramey and Steve Foritano knew that for the photographs to be entered as evidence, they had to be shown to the jury. Wellman objected to the court that Ramey was trying to prejudice the jurors with these gruesome photos. Judge Fenton overruled and allowed them to be entered as evidence and shown to the jurors. As the photographs were passed from juror to juror, the expressions on the faces of the jurors told the story of their impact. One juror looked as though she was going to be physically sick. Another juror just shook his head as he passed the photos on.

TESTIMONY RESUMED on Monday morning, May 10th. DCI criminologist Robert Harvey was called to the stand. He was the specialist who examined, tested and compared the bullet jackets and shell casings recovered at the Drake Diner with others submitted as evidence in the case. Harvey testified that the bullet jackets and shell casings from the diner had unique markings created during firing and ejection from a rare .44 caliber magnum semi-automatic handgun known as a Grizzly. The weapon was manufactured by the Lawrence A. Robinson Company of Utah. He also said that only two types of semi-automatic handguns can handle the .44 Magnum shell – the Desert Eagle and the Grizzly. L.A.R. Manufacturing sent a .44 Grizzly to the Des Moines Police to show what the actual gun looked like and to be introduced as evidence, but Wellman objected and the handgun was not allowed as evidence. It was returned to the Utah manufacturer. Instead, a photograph of a .44 Magnum L.A.R. Grizzly was introduced.

Asked by Jim Ramey if any of the other rounds tested by him matched the Drake Diner bullets and casings, he said they did. Asked which, he said the shell casings from Joseph White's apartment in Seattle; the rounds recovered from the floor at 1517 Washington Avenue and the shooting at 1344 22nd Street were all fired by the gun used at the Drake Diner.

The next prosecution witness was the owner of the Grizzly, Roger Cline. Dressed in a black shirt and trousers, with a dark beard - a mountain of a man - he walked past Joseph White' s seat and gave him an icy glance. Then he took the oath and took the stand. Ramey asked him his name and asked him what he did for a living. He answered that he was semi-retired in real estate. Asked if he was familiar with guns he said he was an "active firearms competitor." Ramey asked him if he owned the Grizzly .44 Magnum in question and he said he did. Ramey asked him about it and how it disappeared.

"I bought the gun in April, 1992. My wife and I were gone on the 9th, 10th, 11th of October, 1992. We went to our cabin in the mountains. After we returned, I noticed it missing on the 15th and reported it on the 23rd."

"Anything else missing, Mr. Cline?"

"I also reported missing a shoulder holster, three loaded clips and $2,500 worth of jewelry."

Ramey asked Mr. Cline how much the gun weighed. He answered, "I don't know for sure but it is very strong, very high powered."

Immediately following her father's testimony, Johanna Cline took the stand. As she walked up to take her seat to testify, people noticed that Joseph White watched her intensely. She ignored his attempts to get her attention and avoided making eye contact with him during her testimony. She testified that she got to know Joseph White briefly through a friend and that he was at her parent's house on one night, October 10th, from 2:30 a.m. until approximately 6:00 a.m.. When asked by prosecutor Ramey if White was ever out of her sight during that time, she said she was in her bedroom alone for about forty minutes. Ramey asked her about her father discovering the missing items; did she think to tell him about Joseph White? She said, "No, I didn't think about it." Asked if he wanted to cross-examine her, John Wellman declined. Jim Rowley heard her testimony and laughed to himself. Based on what her friends in Washington State had told police, there was a lot more testimony that would have made interesting cross examination by Jim Ramey. Prosecutors wanted the opportunity to delve further into the romantic relationship she had with Joe White. Wellman wanted no part of that for obvious reasons. Johanna Cline lowered her head as she left the witness stand, exchanging eye contact with no one. She was escorted from the courthouse, accompanied by her father and sheriff's deputies.

The court took a morning stretch break following Johanna Cline's testimony. Family members of both sides gathered in the courthouse halls and quietly talked. Some went outside to have a cigarette and watch the activity outside. Media vehicles were parked up and down the streets surrounding the building. Parking was hard to find. Lyle Burnett, Tim's twin brother, went outside and walked around the courthouse to pass the time and think, as was his routine.

FOLLOWING THE BREAK, Kent, Washington police officer Russell Walker testified that he worked bike patrol with his partner in the Kent housing area known as Applegate Apartments. They were responding to a call from Mr. Terry Brew, the manager, that loud shots had been fired sounding like they came from the roof of the building where officers knew Joseph White and his mother lived - apartment D105. Mr. Brew said the shots were in rapid succession and it sounded like shell casings were landing in the building's gutters. The officers thought that if White had a gun, they wanted it.

They went to White's apartment and were allowed in. He was there along with another black male juvenile. They asked him about the gun and he said he had no knowledge of a gun. His mother, Sharon James, arrived home and gave them permission to search the apartment. Walker accessed the roof through Joe White's bedroom, went up on the complex roof and found one spent .44 shell casing in the gutter. He went back down to White's bedroom and the officers found the shoulder holster rig with a clip in it and another spent .44 shell on the floor. Walker then asked Joseph White about it and he answered that it wasn't illegal to have those items and he denied knowledge of any gun. The officers issued him a juvenile appearance card and made an appointment for him to come in. He did not come in for his appointment later as scheduled. When the Brews saw the holster rig the officers were carrying out from the apartment that day, they said when the shots were fired earlier, they walked a short distance from the building to get a look at the roof area and they saw that shoulder holster on the roof at that time.

The prosecution continued by calling Sharon James, Joseph White's mother, to establish when they had moved to Washington State and when she brought him to Des Moines to live with relatives. She said, "November something." Detective Bill Boggs testified next about the discovery of the stolen gun in the Seattle area and their investigation. Lt. Jobe's testimony followed Boggs and was cross-examined by Wellman concerning other suspects in the case, among them Jeremy Spenser and Andre Jenkins.

An interesting prosecution tactic was at work in the courtroom: Testimony from head investigator Jim Rowley could have had tremendous implications on the outcome of the trial depending on what questions were asked of him, how he answered them in graphic detail and how they were presented before the jury. John Wellman wanted to have Ramey call Rowley as a prosecution witness, leaving the door open to a possibly severe cross-examination by Wellman based on his fresh prosecution testimony. Wellman wanted to grill detective Rowley concerning the informants who put the authorities on Jo-Jo White's trail. Each morning, prosecutor Ramey laid a folder half full of blank paper in the prosecution's area of the table. It was plainly marked "Rowley." Wellman's paralegal, who had been with him for twenty years, saw the file and whispered to John Wellman, who was blind, that it appeared Rowley would be testifying soon for the prosecution. Wellman would prepare his cross but the prosecution finally rested their case without calling him to the stand, much to the chagrin of defense counsel. Wellman would now be forced to call Rowley as a hostile witness for the defense.

JOHN WELLMAN began his defense Tuesday, the following morning. Seventeen defense witnesses testified: Seven witnesses said the killer wore a ski mask. Ray Slater, 22, a Drake basketball player, testified that he and Kevin Murphy were leaving the diner. He said he opened the door for a man carrying a black semi-automatic pistol. He said the man was wearing a mask and this man walked between him and Kevin Murphy. Slater said he watched him as he walked to the cash register and shot a blond-headed woman.

On cross-examination, Ramey asked Slater what color the mask was. He answered he wasn't sure. Ramey asked what else he could remember about the mask. Slater answered nothing. Ramey asked if he remembered telling police on the night of the murder that the mask was gray with eye holes cut in it. Slater did not remember.

Jim Ramey slowly walked back to his seat at the table and silently read to himself from a yellow legal pad on his table. He then turned to Ray Slater and said, "Are you sure you saw the gunman shoot a blond woman?"

Slater looked at him coolly and answered, "Yes."

Ramey hesitated momentarily and said, "Well, she wasn't blond, as evidence presented has shown, she had dark hair." Slater's stare turned angry and he said his attention was focused on the gun. Slater was excused. The next three defense witnesses cross-examined on their eye-witness testimony, all Drake basketball players, Kevin Murphy, Adrian Gray and Marvin King testified the killer's mask was navy blue, gray and black.

Defense counsel called two witnesses who claimed to have been with Jo-Jo White in the home on Carpenter at the time of the Drake Diner murders. White's cousin, Dora White, and his uncle, Gerald James, both testified, under oath, that they saw him waking up from a nap minutes after the killings occurred. John Wellman finished the day's testimony with Des Moines Police officers and their investigation of other suspects in the case.

Isaac Newsome testified first on Wednesday. He testified that he was a member of the Black Gangster Disciples and gang members were having a party on November 15, 1992, the night he was shot from outside the house. He testified that Vice Lord Jeremy Spencer came up to him later on and apologized for shooting him. Spenser denied saying that on the prosecution's cross-examination when he testified.

Reluctantly, John Wellman called case head investigator Jim Rowley to the witness stand for the defense. He asked him if he remembered writing a police report stating that there was a resemblance between Alf Freddy Clark and the composite the department was using in the case. Rowley admitted he did at the time, then quickly added that the gap in the teeth in the following and final composite resembled Joseph White, not Clark. Wellman immediately, angrily objected to the last statement made by Rowley. He asked the court and jury to disregard it. Judge Fenton allowed it to stand. Wellman was furious. He followed up by asking Rowley if the police paid Tamara Turner two thousand dollars to give them information. Rowley said that she had asked for the money but no money was ever given to her. Wellman was quick to dismiss Rowley from any further testimony in their behalf.

As had been the case for much of the proceedings, Joseph White's family sat at the east end of the courtroom. The Burnett family sat on the west end of the courtroom. The McGrane family was not present. Prosecution witness Scott Birrer sat in the middle row and listened intently to every word. He glanced over at Joseph White's mother who seemed nervous.

JOHN WELLMAN was going to allow Joseph Hodges White, Jr. to testify on his own behalf. He felt that to portray Joe, in his own words, as a teenager surrounded by tough circumstances might save this young man's future. His gut feeling was that the jury might see him as a young individual railroaded by the system trying to solve the Drake Diner murders. Everyone involved in the case, including the media and courtroom observers, knew that Thursday, May 13th would be the day that Joe White had an opportunity to explain his way out of the case the prosecution had built against him. There were sixty observers in the courtroom, additional people including reporters in the outside hallway and extra sheriff's deputies both inside and outside the courthouse. The local television stations interrupted their daily programming to carry Joseph White's testimony live.

Joseph White was escorted into the courtroom by several armed deputies. He was dressed in a rust colored suit with a black shirt and matching rust tie. He sat at the defense area of the long table. He turned around scanning the gallery, looked at family members and friends and smiled broadly. As proceedings began, White took the witness stand. Under direct examination, John Wellman asked him about his life – where he had lived, where he grew up, where he attended school and when he lived in Washington State. As part of his end-run defense strategy, John Wellman asked him if he was in a gang in Washington. White said he was a "Blood." Counsel then asked him if he brought the .44 Magnum Grizzly to Des Moines. Joe White said that he did. He was asked if he stole the gun from Roger Cline. White denied it and blamed the theft of Roger Cline's Grizzly on Marlin Curry, his friend who was at the Cline house with him and the girls that night.

Wellman continued, "Joe, did you fire this gun in your apartment there in Kent, Washington?"

Seemingly annoyed by the question, he replied, "No, I did not." Wellman asked him about the circumstances surrounding that report. Joe White answered, "Marlin Curry had the gun. I told him to get it out of here and he shot it in my house and the

bullet flew out the window." Wellman asked him how it was that
he brought the .44 Grizzly to Des Moines.

"It was a going away gift."

"When you got to Des Moines, did you have the gun with
you after that?"

"No, somebody else had it all the time. Then I sold it to
Jeremy Spenser after about a week for $300."

Christa, Wellman's paralegal, whispered quietly to him,
Wellman nodded and asked Joe White, "Did you have any other
guns here in Des Moines?"

"I had a silver Colt .45 that I bought from a guy on the street
for $50."

"Where did you keep it?"

"Here and there, here and there, somethin' like that." White
said he kept it at Tamara's house at 1517 Washington. He said
about fifteen people kept guns there since it was a Vice Lords
house. Asked about where he was when Isaac Newsome was
shot, he told the court he was at home. Asked where he was
when the Drake Diner murders occurred he said he was at home
sleeping. Asked by John Wellman about the gun being fired
into the floor at 1517 Washington, White said he thought it was
the same night that they went to the hotel. Asked why he was
handling the Grizzly when it discharged, he said he hadn't seen
the gun for a while and "wanted to see it for old time sake."
Wellman asked him if he lied to the police. He answered that he
did - to keep them off of him as a suspect. He told police he had
never seen the gun and he made up the name "David" during the
police interrogation to protect Jeremy Spenser. Wellman then
concluded his direct examination and the court took a recess.

DURING THE RECESS, outside of the presence of the jury,
Judge Fenton asked Jim Ramey if he anticipated "going into"
drawings and writings confiscated from Joseph White while
he was in the Polk County Jail. John Wellman and the
paralegal had copies of the drawings and writings in question.

She explained them to Wellman as best she could. Judge Fenton sat back slowly on the bench and asked Ramey what the relevance was of the evidence he intended to introduce.

Ramey answered the judge's question in an angry tone, "The drawings and writings show the defendant is lying! His drawings show him as a 'Blood,' in gang colors. They show him with GUNS – automatic pistols and shotguns. Pictures of HIMSELF, his initials and his name written on the pages, himself in a mask, gun in *right hand* and cash in the left hand! A 'CK' – A CRIP KILLER! Guns pointed AT PEOPLE'S HEADS!"

John Wellman listened and smiled. He said that what a person writes or draws after five months in jail is of no relevance here - totally collateral. Ramey approached the bench and gave the judge copies of the evidence, marked by exhibit number. He walked Judge Fenton through the most damaging of the drawings showing gang participation, guns, robbery, killing and mayhem. The judge took his time going through the drawings. He looked over at the defendant, silent at the defense table, looked back at Jim Ramey and said he would allow the evidence, but warned Ramey "try to limit the number of pictures and exhibits you use." Ramey thanked the court.

When the court reconvened, Joseph White returned to the witness stand. Ramey asked him if he had stolen the .44 Grizzly belonging to Roger Cline. He denied it and said that Marlin Curry was the culprit. A noticeably unbelieving Ramey asked him if he noticed any bulge in Marlin Curry's clothing that would have concealed a large handgun and all of the associated items that were stolen at the Cline's home that night. Joseph White said he didn't notice anything.

He was asked whether he had ever fired the .44 Grizzly and he denied it. Ramey quickly reminded him that he admitted firing a round into the floor at 1517 Washington. He said that he *had* fired the gun that night. Ramey then asked if he shot the Grizzly at his apartment in Kent, Washington when the police came and investigated. White denied it. Ramey asked him if he was saying that the Kent, Washington police officer, Russell Walker, lied on the witness stand about his report. White said that Officer Walker did lie. White added that he never gave Walker and his partner permission to enter and search the apartment – "they just barged right in." Ramey slowed his pace and again asked White if the officer was lying to the court in his testimony. White said that he was.

JIM RAMEY, in an accentuated gesture, snatched up the folder containing the jail drawings from the prosecution table. He gave copies to Wellman's paralegal and approached the bench. John Wellman's assistant was quietly explaining to Wellman what she saw in these jailhouse drawings as quickly as she could. The prosecutor got Jo-Jo White's attention, walked over to him in the witness stand and handed him a picture.

"Joseph, it says J.O.E.W., doesn't it?"

"Yes."

"And you are holding what in your right hand?"

"An automatic pistol."

Ramey turned to the jury, "With shell casings popping out! This is exhibit 65." 65 was admitted by the court.

He handed White another drawing, "Drawn in the Polk County Jail?"

"Yes, it was."

"Holding a 12 gauge shotgun, firing at Crips. Exhibit 66!" 66 was admitted.

White was handed another drawing, "Masked gunman, gun in right hand. Exhibit 67!" 67 was admitted.

And so it went for exhibits 68 through 72. Drawings were admitted with the shooter in a hooded sweatshirt, "Bloods" on the do-rags worn on the shooters' heads in the drawings, Aunt Zella's phone number on the pages and more portrayals of the shooter, in the jailhouse drawings, as a right handed shooter.

Ramey continued asserting that Joseph White didn't really want to tell them about the party at the Holiday Inn Downtown.

White said that he didn't remember it. "If they only would have asked me about it, I would have told them but I didn't remember it." Ramey walked over to the windows in the courtroom looking over the street outside, and while looking outside he said that White had testified that he, the defendant, didn't remember times and dates accurately. White spoke up in the affirmative, agreeing.

"But you remembered 6:30 on the night of the Drake Diner murders. Every time you went in the kitchen, you looked at the clock? What kind of a sandwich was it?" He answered he didn't remember. "And Detective Roth asked you if you, *if you,* had been around guns. You denied it repeatedly! You have admitted lying. You've testified you didn't remember the 1517 Washington incident. You've denied saying to Roth that you said it was a .357 revolver!" Ramey slowed his pace at that point and said, "You didn't ever admit the gun came from you. You could have identified the Grizzly."

White said, "I would have told them the night they arrested me if they would have asked me."

Ramey looked Joseph White in the eye and said, "You told them it *wasn't* a Grizzly." Ramey continued, "When you came to Des Moines on November 5th, when did you take the gun out of your luggage?"

"When I went to my aunt's."

"You had $300 dollars when you came to town?"

"Yes, I did."

"What did you spend it on?"

"I didn't spend it. I invested it in somethin'."

Jim Ramey paused with a questioning expression on his face. "What did you invest it in?"

White replied, "That's irrelevant. You asked me if I spent it. I invested it."

Ramey, hardly able to conceal his curiosity, said, "*In what?*"

Obviously annoyed by this questioning, Joseph White replied, "Stocks!"

"What?" Jim Ramey could hardly conceal his pleasure with that answer, "Stocks, bonds, certificates?"

"Stocks!"

Ramey shook his head. "What stocks could you have invested it in?"

"Can't say, man - my memory."

"L.A.R. Manufacturing?"

"No!"

Ramey's expression changed to one of obvious disbelief and delight in the direction the questioning was going. "Well, if you're a stock investor and the police asked you about the money at the hotel – why didn't you tell them it was a dividend from your stock?"

White answered, "Basically, I did. But I knew they knew what I was talkin' about. And why would I say somethin' like that anyway? I knew I had the money!"

Ramey's expression became serious and he nodded, "You were dealing dope, that's what you mean."

Jo-Jo White's supporters in the courtroom began laughing and disrupting the proceedings. Without looking around into the gallery, Jim Ramey requested, "Your honor, can we ask the people not to be clapping and applauding?" Judge Fenton told the spectators to refrain from any outbursts or he would clear the courtroom. Following that, Ramey asked him, "You don't want to tell us where the money came from, do you?" White said he did not and Ramey rested.

John Wellman followed. "Joseph, are the pictures you drew in the Polk County Jail pictures of yourself?"

"No."

Wellman continued, "And people who grow up in a gang culture, do they snitch and cooperate with the police, Joe?"

"No." Wellman rested.

Ramey asked him, "Joe, do people who grow up in a gang culture murder?"

"Yes."

"Do they rob?"

"Yes."

"Can they be cold blooded?"

"Yes." Ramey rested.

John Wellman came back one more time, "Joe, is he talking about you?"

"No." Wellman rested and Joseph White was excused from the stand. As he was led from the courthouse back to the Polk County Jail, he saw his mother and waived and smiled at her. As he looked in the opposite direction he caught the glance of Lyle Burnett. Lyle's icy stare was met by one of Joe White's own.

SATURDAY, THE 22nd, was the day of final arguments. Thousands of people on a weekend day off tuned in cable TV to watch the attorney's arguments and exchange. The courtroom was packed. Phyllis Burnett spoke to a reporter early that morning and said that she believed Joe White was the one who killed Tim and she should despise him for it. She continued and said that she just couldn't and it wouldn't bring Tim back or do any good anyway.

The courtroom was brought to order. Judge Fenton read the instructions to the jury. He reviewed the charges – one count of 1st degree robbery and two counts of 1st degree murder. He emphasized that the state must prove its case. He reminded the jury that there was a presumption of innocence to be considered. He slowly emphasized that the verdict must be based on evidence *beyond a reasonable doubt*. He finished and allowed Polk County Attorney Jim Ramey to begin summarizing the state's case. The different styles of James Ramey and John Wellman became clear during final arguments. Wellman's arguments were presented in a softer, deft fashion. Ramey, on the other hand, seemed borderline angry at times, emphatic, dead serious and bellicose to drive his points home.

Ramey stood and moved before the jury box, positioning a four foot tall easel within easy view of the jurors. The chart/ calendar page they were viewing was an October – November – December calendar tracing the recent history of this L.A.R. Grizzly .44 Magnum semi-automatic. Ramey, satisfied with the positioning of the easel, turned to the jury and began. "Closing arguments are very important for a variety of reasons. Primarily, it gives both sides the final opportunity to present their best case to the jury. It capsulates days of testimony, sometimes long days, and puts them into an understandable frame for you." He hesitated purposefully, looked at Joseph White, looked back toward the jurors and said, "If this is not a case of first degree murder – then what can this possibly be? This man came into the Drake Diner with a .44 Magnum and shot Cara McGrane point blank. And when Tim Burnett came running to help her, he shot him, too. Even though the police made the arrest of the defendant in one week, they kept investigating. They did not stop or rest. They kept following up leads and tips. Even though it was by all descriptions 'a speedy arrest,' they continued gathering evidence. Detective Boggs – they knew it was a Grizzly. The killer left evidence at the scene: shell casings and the bullets. The casings told us what we were looking for – an L.A.R. Grizzly .44 Magnum automatic."

The prosecutor hesitated and pointed on the calendar exhibit to Saturday, October 10th. "Roger Cline had an L.A.R. Grizzly .44 Magnum automatic. He was a shooter and kept his spent shell casings. We were lucky. The Clines went to their country cabin for that weekend. Their daughter brought Joe White to their home against their wishes and he stole Roger Cline's gun. He killed two people with Roger Cline's .44 Grizzly." Ramey then pointed to October 17th and said, "A .44 Magnum fired on the apartment roof. The police are summoned. They talk to Joe White and he denies everything. The police find a .44 Magnum casing on the roof in the rain gutter. They confiscate casings, a loaded .44 clip and a pistol harness in Joe White's apartment.

You know what Joe says? He blames it on Marlin, his buddy. Marlin stole the gun at Cline's house and brought it to Joe White's to shoot it."

Jim Ramey stopped momentarily, looked at the floor, looked at the jury and wrote five bold letters across the top of the easel sheet. S-O-D-D-I. "Ladies and gentleman, this is known as the SODDI Defense – Some Other Dude Did It. Some other dude brought it over to Joe's apartment. Joe says he told him he didn't want to be around no gun, but some other dude left the harness, clip and shells at Joe's. He admitted lying to the police. Kent Police Department – good work." He pointed to the calendar again and said, "He was at Cline's on the 10th. He fired the gun at the apartment on the 17th. He moves to Des Moines around November 9th. He can't deny he brought the gun to Des Moines." He stopped with a slight smile on his face and added, "Marlin gave him the .44 as a going away gift – Joe, the guy who left this gang life behind: a gift – a $1,000 handgun."

Jim Ramey points again to calendar, "November 15th, Isaac Newsome is shot. Two shots and two casings are recovered. Des Moines Police now have one case involving a .44 Magnum." Pointing lower on the calendar, "November 29th, two homicides and the robbery of the Drake Diner." He slows the pace, "We know that on the 26th and the 27th Joe White had a large black handgun. But that caused Joe White a problem. So he had to buy another gun – a .45." Ramey smiles, "We don't know where that gun is, of course. Remember, he's not into gang stuff anymore but he tells friends 'a real man carries a gun'."

The prosecutor steps away from the chart momentarily and looks at the expressions of the jurors. After a moment he looks back to the calendar, he points, and says, "On the 29th after the murders, he has the gun he supposedly sold, again at 1517 Washington and discharges it into the floor. Joe says it wasn't the same day. He tells police it was the day before they went to the Holiday Inn, Wednesday or Thursday. Barbara Hogan and Tammy Turner testified it was the night of the Drake Diner killings. Joe White tried to dig up the bullets from the floor."

RAMEY LOOKED over at Joseph White at the defense table and shook his head. "When the Des Moines Police heard about what happened at 1517 Washington the night of the killings, they went up there with a search warrant and recovered a bullet from the ducts of the furnace that matched the weapon used in the Drake Diner murders." Ramey stopped intentionally and pointed to White, "No witnesses have identified anyone else as the killer! Not one other person has identified anyone else! Consider the evidence."

The prosecutor stopped, walked to the window for a moment, turned and walked back over to the jury box. "People have said the killer had a mask on. But this can be reconciled by the eyewitness testimony of people who described the killer's features. Consider Scott Birrer, standing across a counter, talking to the woman. Birrer described the killer's features. He was across the counter talking to his friend when this young man came up and interrupted and killed his friend. He describes the features. He saw the gun to her head. He describes the aspects of what happened. He saw the gun to her head - didn't think he was going to shoot when he fired." Ramey slowed down again for emphasis, "Scott Birrer was one of the few people in the Drake Diner that night who showed some degree of composure. He ran out of the diner not to get away but to follow him. Scott Birrer wanted to chase this man but didn't want to catch him. Good idea. He went back inside the diner and he told people to sit down. He told witnesses that the police were going to want to talk with them about what happened. He'd had lifeguard training and he went to help Tim Burnett but there was no helping him."

"Let's look at Dontrell Ducker – the young busboy who passed right by Joe White. He was thirteen feet away and he looked him right in the eye. He knew him. He saw the murders.

When they assembled a composite picture of the killer, he *insisted* on the gap in the teeth. He said, 'When I heard the name Joe White on TV, I knew it was the guy I knew.' Joe had changed. It wasn't the same kid he knew. The other witness, Jonas Chladek, again, was right there. Fifteen years old, making up his own mind, could identify him. He pointed him out in the police photo lineup as scared as he was."

Jim Ramey turned, looked at Joseph White, then turned and looked back toward the jurors making individual eye contact with each juror. "Isn't it strange that these three people could pick out Joe White who says he's the wrong man – who was at Roger Cline's house *a thousand miles away*. Of all the people in the whole world, they pick out the one guy who had been there when the .44 Grizzly was stolen – *Isn't that a coincidence?* They picked out the same guy who brought the gun to Des Moines and fired it at 1517 Washington on the night of the Drake Diner killings."

Slowing his pace again for emphasis, Ramey talked about reasonable doubt and the importance of the jurors conviction on their feelings. "I'm going to ask you all to do something difficult. Have as much guts as Scott Birrer, Dontrell Ducker and Jonas Chladek. We need your opinion on this to convict him. Yes, he's seventeen, but it's great police work and a strong case." Looking back toward the defense table and pointing, "Joe White is going to lay these things off on anyone he can!" Referring more casually to the easel chart map he pointed to 2212 Carpenter, where Joe White lived, and showed its relationship to the location of the Drake Diner. He then pointed a block north of the Carpenter residence and followed the alley with his pointer, "Isaac Newsome was shot right here."

He laid the pointer down, smiled, shook his head and turned to jurors again. "He didn't invest in stocks. Witnesses have testified he never had any money. But then he had money to rent the suite at the Holiday Inn. He testified he had $70. The others testified he had a lot more. So, before the robbery on

Sunday, he didn't have any money. When asked for cigarette money around 6:15, he didn't have any money. Friday, when asked by Barbara Hogan for five dollars, he didn't have any money. Sunday, at 6:15, he didn't have any money; at 6:30, he didn't have any money; at 6:45, he didn't have any money; at 7:00, he had $1,000. He had just killed two innocent people to get it." Ramey stopped and looked over at Joseph White and shook his head, "But he didn't have to shoot them." He put an 11X14 photo of an L.A.R. Grizzly on the easel for the jury to see. Examining the photo he said, "With one of these, to rob, all you have to do *is show it*. But on that night he used it." Looking at the jurors, he said, "Show some courage." Again, he turned to Joseph White and pointed directly at him, "Joseph Hodges White, Junior is the murderer. Thank you" The court's morning recess followed.

CHRISTA, JOHN WELLMAN'S legal assistant, guided the blind attorney to the right position facing the jury. He did not have the luxury of being able to make eye contact with each juror. In a quieter, metered tone, John Wellman began, "Let's talk for awhile about reason and logic and common sense and apply these principles. Analyze what I say. The State of Iowa has the burden of proof here. The state possesses the resources, the assets and the personnel to investigate crimes such as this. These were brought to bear on the case involving the Drake Diner. They used the evidence and the facts to come up with a *theory*. The theory was that Joseph Hodges White, Jr. was the killer. Jurors, do you have all the evidence or just what supports and is consistent with the theory? If there are facts that are inconsistent with the theory, then the theory fails."

"Joseph White was arrested because he discharged a gun and the witnesses who picked him out – one 70% sure, one 50% sure and one between two and five and because he went to the Holiday Inn. It was tremendous police work uncovering that Joe White brought the gun to Des Moines. That is not in dispute here. Had that not been disclosed by good police work, you and I know that Joe White wouldn't have admitted bringing the gun to the State of Iowa. Remember, witness Harvey from the state, couldn't say who fired the gun that hit Isaac Newsome or who fired it at the Drake Diner. *Therefore* . . . therefore, Joseph White brought the gun to Des Moines; therefore, Joseph White shot Isaac Newsome; therefore, Joseph White robbed the Drake Diner. That's their theory. You see, their chain of circumstances and connections has to be intact. If the chain is broken the theory fails."

"Isaac Newsome says it was someone else who shot him but the police department didn't care about that until after the Drake Diner murders. Officer Rowley testified that nobody other than Joseph White had possession of the gun but witnesses said that fifteen to twenty Vice Lords kept their guns at 1517 Washington. So how does he know what he said to be true? Reasonable doubt arises from failure of the evidence to convince you. Many witnesses said that the man had a mask - a few said he didn't. They choose to disregard the many for the few."

John Wellman stopped momentarily to let his words sink in. "Please recall the 911 tape – pandemonium, screaming – are eyewitness recantifications out of that environment enough to make a finding beyond a reasonable doubt? Mr. Ramey asks you to listen to selected witnesses only. Scott Birrer picks out my client six months after the fact, only 100% sure if he can see the man again. The photo line-up is suggestive – Joe White is the only one with a hooded sweatshirt."

"Let's look at the witnesses. Lisa Taylor tells police she can't ID him but picks him out in court. Folks, people see what they want to see." Wellman turns to the easel chart now showing a list of witnesses at the diner that night. "All the witnesses names on this chart are co-workers, friends, somebody who dated one of the victims. That doesn't say they are bad people. As a friend or co-worker, when the police announce they caught the person responsible, we want it to be the person who did it. We are talking about psychological factors here – not reason and logic. Janet Pittman remembers the gap in the teeth. Is she ID'ing the teeth or Joe White?"

John Wellman's ease and quiet manner seem compelling to jurors who listen attentively. "Is Joe White the only black youth in Des Moines with a gap in his teeth? Dontrell Ducker wasn't sure about the gap in his teeth at first, then he's 100% sure? The state contends that the gap in the teeth is right because Joseph White has a gap in his teeth. Scott Birrer testified that he picked my client out of the line-up immediately. Officer Westover said it took some time before picking him out and then he said he was 70% sure. At Drake, 70% is a 'C.' We'll give him a 'C.' Maybe, the best witnesses are the ones who don't come to court – that don't have motivation. Think about all the people who saw a ski mask. Ray Slater was a foot away. How do you overlook this? Your government is asking you to do that."

He stops again for a moment, apparently in thought. "People from a different background or race – do we lower the burden of proof for them? We can talk about people who come from a disadvantaged background and have to survive by any means available to them. Often, people in that environment do not readily cooperate with the police. What's to be gained? Here's a young man who has admitted lying to the police." Wellman smiles slightly and shakes his head, "To a young man who said he bought stocks when we knew he was selling drugs. To a young man who had been involved with youth gangs. In rebuttal, Mr. Ramey is going to say that Mr. Wellman said this and Mr. Wellman said that. I feel the weight and responsibility for the young man and you're going to hear a lot more about what a bad person Joe White is."

"One more point that I would like to make: Joseph Hodges White told the police that he was *both-handed,* ambidextrous, when he knew the police were searching for a right-handed killer and he is left-handed. Why would the liar tell the police something like that? We can't sidestep analysis of this evidence. I will sit down. I just ask you to consider what I've said in this serious undertaking. Consider the evidence presented and apply reason and logic and common sense and come to a conclusion that you can leave the courthouse with being *comfortable*, as Mr. Ramey puts it." Christa led John Wellman back to his chair at the defense table and he sat down.

FOLLOWING A RECESS, Jim Ramey began his summation. "Mr. Wellman says I'm going to get up and say that Mr. Wellman said this and that and that this young man is a bad kid. He's the one talking of logic and reason. Mr. Wellman put him on the stand trying to paint him out as a high school kid who happened to, for a while, have a run of bad luck." Jim Ramey stopped, shook his head and looked to the jurors. "He was an Elm Street Piru Blood – a gang member. That is not logic. That is not reason. In their case, when the facts are against you – scream about the facts. When the law is against you – scream about the law. When it seems to work, just scream. Mr. Wellman says your government is *picking on* Joseph White. Give me a break! Picking on him; the police, the eyewitnesses?"

"Keep in mind that after the police had Joe White in custody, they kept investigating. It was only because they kept digging that they found the evidence that implicated the person they already had in custody – Joseph Hodges White, Jr." Ramey suddenly raised the volume of his voice exclaiming, "And Mr. Wellman tells you with absolute candor that you know darn well when Joe White took the witness stand, if Mr. Ramey hadn't been able to absolutely prove that the gun came from Washington with Joe White he would have lied to you about that! That's what he told you just a few minutes ago, folks. I'll admit it to you; if my client hadn't known that that son of a gun from the government over there could prove a case against him, he would have lied. That's just what he just told you. And if Mr. Ramey can't prove it, by George, we'll lie about it! That's what he told you! Mr. Wellman tells you: 'We'll lie if they can't prove it to be an absolute fact."

John Wellman shook his head at the defense table and let out a slightly audible laugh for all to hear. Ramey, angered by that, turned to him, "I'm glad you're amused, Mr. Wellman; I'm not! I am disgusted that an attorney would stand up here and tell you that: that if I can't prove it to you, I'll lie!" Ramey pointed to John Wellman and looked at the jurors, "He is not your government, thank goodness. You all ought to thank goodness! If the other supposed witnesses Mr. Wellman refers to can't identify the suspect, why should I waste your time? There were over forty people in the diner that night. Should we have brought them all in?"

The prosecutor walked over toward Joseph White, looked him in the eye and said, "This man would lie about anything the government thought was important; left-handed – he'd lie; Holiday Inn if it was important – he'd lie; the .44 Grizzly – he'd lie. No one else was identified. I'm not sure who they were planning on pinning this on. This can't be blamed on poor economic conditions of the family that did their best with this young man. Dontrell Ducker grew up in the same environment, but he didn't sell drugs or draw guns 'cause that was all he could do.' No! He got a scholarship to South Dakota University -that's what life can be if you work at it. The difference here is that Joe White believed that being a man comes from carrying a gun. Jurors, we have to say that you can't come to our town and do this. Find him guilty for the common good of us all. And when there is evidence that you have committed this crime – as a government, we say that you are guilty. Thank you."

Chapter Eleven

JUDGE FENTON read the instructions to the jury and they began deliberating. It was Saturday and the first day of deliberation lasted only three hours following the morning's proceedings. Hopes of a near instantaneous verdict were dashed and jurors ended by going to their homes for the weekend to return early Monday.

IT WAS RAINING Monday morning when the 'day detectives' reported in. Jobe walked in to the morning meeting, slapped some paperwork down on the desk and told the assembled detectives that the "Diner" was now up to the jury. He remarked that everything they had thought of to do had been done and then some. "I have never seen anything like this case – ever." But then he continued that the current caseload was still suffering from the manpower drain of that case. He told everyone to forget about the diner and focus on the here-and-now. Rowley, sitting in the back, chuckled to himself.

Jim Rowley went over to his desk following the meeting and thumbed through his cases and paperwork. He had some old continuation follow-up cases to look at and several new cases for follow-up from the weekend including a homicide at 23rd and Forest, near Drake, from late Saturday night that other detectives had worked on that night. The suspect was still currently on the loose. He thought he might know who the shooter was. His calendar for the day included a dentist appointment at 11:00 a.m. and a meeting at the county attorney's office after lunch. He went to the dentist at 11:00 and all the hygienist and the dentist were interested in talking about was the murder, the trial and how long he thought the jury would be out in deliberation. With the dentist's hand in his mouth, he managed to communicate, "I'm not sure on that."

The meeting with assistant county attorney Steve Foritano and child welfare involved a case where the babysitter had allowed a child in her care to fall, injure himself and die as a result of the fall. The police department had investigated the case and felt that there was reasonable doubt concerning the role that the sitter had in what happened to the child – unfortunately very common occurrences and investigations in the world that we live in. But today, with the jury out on the Joseph White case, both Steve Foritano and Jim Rowley had vested interests in listening for news. The meeting lasted until 3:30 and no one had heard anything from the courthouse. Monday ended that way.

On Tuesday, Jim was called to assist on a bank robbery investigation on Merle Hay Road in northwest Des Moines. FBI field agents were already on the scene, along with Des Moines Police, when he arrived with Sgt. Bob Ervin. Jim looked around, checking out the arrangement of the bank and the positioning of the holdup man during the robbery. He listened to two young-looking federal agents questioning the tellers and witnesses. He thought to himself that their questions sounded amateur for law-enforcement professionals. After they finished their interviews, the agents snapped their notebooks closed and walked over to Jim Rowley and Sgt. Ervin. The younger looking of the two agents with the cocky attitude, asked Jim what they made of the "M.O." of the robber. Rowley took a deep breath, sighed, looked around for a moment studying his surroundings and answered, "It looks to me like a white guy with a mask robbed this bank this morning and got away." With that, Jim smiled and he and Sgt. Ervin walked away.

In spite of the media focus on the jury deliberation in the case, Drake area residents tried to keep this attention from scaring people away again. Drake security reported that crime there was low. Alan Cubbage, Drake's marketing director, said there had been no negative impact to recruiting. He said that tuition deposits were up for the freshman class coming to Drake. Drake Diner's Steve Vilmain said that business had lagged some through the winter but it was keeping pace with business from the year before. He said that possibly the most distressing result of the murders to residents was the bad publicity.

The jury, comprised of seven men and five women, continued to deliberate into Wednesday. The Des Moines Register announced that the presiding judge, Ray Fenton, had gone to Canada on a fishing trip. Judge Rodney Ryan was on the bench in his absence. Attorneys said that once the case was in the hands of the jury, it didn't make a lot of difference which judge presided – *the jury* was now in charge of the disposition of the case. Most disturbing to Detective Jim Rowley on Wednesday was the phone call he received that afternoon from his mother, Twyla. She said, "Jim, I watched the whole trial on TV. You arrested the wrong guy. This boy is innocent. This case in the jury's hands is going too long and they're figuring it out." After the third straight day of deliberation, Jim had a hard time sleeping that night.

THURSDAY, MAY 20th, began with Lt. Jobe being stopped outside the police station at 6:45 a.m. by a TV crew and being asked why he thought the jury was still out deciding this case. Did he have any feeling about the length of time? It had been four and a half days. Doesn't this work in Joseph White's favor due to the length of time? Laddie Jobe, in a hurry to get inside, carefully selecting his answers said, "Juries are juries. We've seen them come back in three hours and we've seen them out for a week." As he walked away at a quick pace, the reporter ran alongside and asked him what the result was of the jury that was out for a week before. Jobe continued to walk and said, "I don't have any more to say at this time." The news story that the TV station ran in conjunction with his comments looked at the possibility of White being found not guilty and its effects on the families of the victims and the community at large. White's family members were interviewed and again they stated their contention that Joe White was innocent and the police were looking for a scapegoat to save their reputation at the expense of an innocent boy. They felt that the long deliberation was a sign that the jury was not convinced of Joe White's involvement in the Drake Diner murders.

On Thursday evening, Connie Rowley, Jim's wife, wanted to go out to dinner. She knew that Jim was a bundle of nerves. Their phone had been ringing off the wall with reporters, friends and fellow officers. Jim had worked quite a hard week with the diner case always on his mind. He was late getting home that night and told Connie that he was really tired and wanted to just stay home and relax. She agreed and the two ended up going to bed before the ten o'clock news.

TWENTY-EIGHT HOURS of deliberation ended on the morning of Friday, May 21st, 1993. An announcement of a reached verdict was made to the court. The news media couldn't get the announcement out fast enough. The verdict would be read at approximately 1:00 p.m.

By 11:00 a.m., the Polk County Courthouse was jammed. News crews were setting up equipment and noon broadcast teams were preparing for their live noon coverage knowing that throngs of people were tuning in. Regular programming was interrupted through the verdict of the trial on most stations. Des Moines Police and the Polk County Sheriff's Office had scores of uniformed and plain clothed officers assigned to monitor activity in and around the courthouse through the reading of the verdict.

Just prior to 1:00 p.m., six deputies escorted Joseph White to his seat in the courtroom. Robert Rigg, a lawyer for the public defender's office would be representing White for the verdict. Rigg entered the courtroom and approached Joe White. They shook hands and he introduced himself. Asked why John Wellman was not going to be in court for the conclusion of the trial, Rigg said to Joe White that Wellman had a serious heart condition and he did not go to verdicts. Joe White suddenly looked disappointed. Judge Fenton had returned from his Canada fishing trip earlier that morning and was already seated on the bench. The courtroom gallery was full to capacity and quiet. Lyle Burnett opened the door and moved to a spot in the back where family members made him a small space. White's family members whispered among themselves quietly. His mother and grandmother sat with their heads bowed, possibly in prayer. Jim Ramey then entered the courtroom and took his seat. None of Cara McGrane's family attended.

Judge Fenton warned those in the courtroom not to make any noises or disturbances during the reading of the verdict. He said, "This has been a highly emotional situation right from the beginning. Emotions are running high on both sides. The jury has deliberated for part of six days. They have worked hard and they command your respect when they get here." At 1:08 p.m., the jury, composed of eleven whites and one black, entered the courtroom and moved to their seats. None looked at Joseph White as they entered. William Thompson, the jury foreman approached the bench and handed the judge their decision.

Fenton carefully examined the sheet he had been handed. He looked to the prosecution table and he then looked at Joseph White. He read, "Joseph Hodges White, first to the charge of armed robbery, the jury finds you guilty." His mother, Sharon White, stared straight ahead with no expression. "Then," the judge continued, "to the two counts of first degree murder, the jury also finds you guilty as charged." Many of White's family members and friends bowed their heads in silence.

First to leave the courtroom were the jury members, escorted by sheriff's deputies. Following that, Joseph White was taken immediately from the courthouse back to the Polk County Jail. Jim Ramey was ushered to his office by armed deputies. Others in the courtroom filed out into the hall. Zella Berry was crying and holding her hand over her mouth as she left. Court attendants took members of White's family across the hall to another office to talk with Robert Rigg. Lyle Burnett had no expression during the reading of the verdict but immediately following the verdict he vaulted up the courthouse stairs to the Polk County Attorney's Office. There he hugged and thanked assistant prosecutor Steve Foritano for a job well done. Jim Ramey was advised by deputies to remain in his office until the courthouse was emptied. He had received death threats if White was found guilty.

Family members and friends of Joe White's congregated outside the courthouse and spoke with the media who were waiting for their reactions. His grandmother, Dora James, said, "How they found him guilty is beyond me. I'm very appalled." Picketers carried signs that said White was railroaded. But employees and friends at the Drake Diner broke into hugs and tears as they watched on TV as the verdict was read. Soon after that the diner received a threatening phone call. Drake Diner kitchen manager Mark De Van, who knew the White family, said there was too much lying going on among the witnesses for Joe White. He said, "I don't think they did him any favors."

Word of the guilty verdict had already made its way to the county jail across the street from the courthouse by the time Joseph White was returned. Two deputies escorted him back to his cell. He wore an angry expression on his face – an expression whose ferocity he would not have wanted to display in court. He walked slowly to his bunk and sat down. Cellmate Carlos Rivera said, "It sounds like they fucked you, brother." White looked over at him and said, "My fucking lawyer didn't have the balls to show up. He knew – he fucking knew!"

As Robert Rigg said earlier, John Wellman didn't attend verdicts. It was too hard on his heart. Wellman told reporters that he thought Joe White was innocent. He seemed to them to be very upset with the verdict. He reacted to questions by saying, "I'm left wondering if there wasn't something else I could have done. At this point I'm filled with a sense of despair and self-doubt. We will be starting to prepare for an appeal."

Reactions to the jury's guilty verdict were unfortunately but predictably split along racial lines. Dennis Green, who sat in for part of the trial, said that having eleven whites and only one black person on the jury should not have been permitted. "You put six black folks and six whites on that jury and Joe White would be a free man now." Confidential sources told WHO-TV that eight of the jurors were convinced early of White's guilt and that the last holdout juror had just come over before the verdict was announced. Asked for his reaction to the verdict, Assistant Chief Bill McCarthy said, "We're pleased but we're not celebrating. You can't look at this kid and not realize how his life is ruined." Lead detective Jim Rowley said, "The jury convicted a young man who believed that all power comes from the barrel of a gun." Rowley had been told that the jury had a verdict at least a day prior to the announcement but some jurors were in fear for their lives given the guilty verdict. Jim Ramey said that he wasn't surprised by what he considered 'a true and just verdict'. He added, "People have called here saying I should be killed." Following a series of threatening calls that followed the verdict, police were assigned to guard the homes of several people connected to the case including a prosecutor, several key prosecution witnesses, a jury member and the Drake Diner itself.

The following Sunday, the Black Ministerial Alliance led a march through downtown Des Moines that ended at the east door of the Polk County Courthouse. Marchers were convinced that Joseph White had been railroaded. News crews covered the event. John Wellman quickly announced that he planned to file a motion for a new trial mainly based on the discredited testimony of Jodie Guill, who said the man who ran in front of her car at 24th and University that night was Joseph White. In the meantime, Judge Fenton announced that sentencing would be scheduled for Wednesday, July 14th. Days later, Judge Fenton ruled on Wellman's motion and a document filed by prosecutor Steve Foritano. Rowley's police report contained information that discredited Jodie Guill's story – Wellman said he hadn't read it. The judge ruled that Jodie Guill's testimony was not an essential contribution to the jury's decision in the White case – the guilty verdict stood.

Epilogue

THE WORST FLOOD in recorded Iowa history took place during July 1993. The Des Moines Waterworks was breached with floodwater. Hundreds of thousands of people were without power or clean water for days, some for as long as a month. The flooding caused billions of dollars in damage and left hundreds homeless. The Des Moines Grand Prix was cancelled July 12th. There seemed to be no end in sight to the continuing rains that soaked not only Iowa but also the entire Midwest. It was against this backdrop that Joseph Hodges White, Jr. was sentenced to life in prison without chance of parole. His life sentence began on July 20th, 1993 at the Iowa Correctional Facility at Clarinda - undergoing evaluation. He was transferred to the maximum-security prison at Ft. Madison where he reportedly became one of the most violent and disruptive inmates in the correctional system.

The family of Tim Burnett tried to return to a fairly normal life following everything that happened. Tim's sister Paulette said that thoughts of Tim were with her constantly. Lyle was lost without his twin brother and decided to go back to Arizona. Their mother, Phyllis, sold her home and went to Arizona with Lyle.

Detective Chief Bill McCarthy stated in a report to the public that the Des Moines Police Department had spent over 3,700 hours on the case and the cost was estimated at over $75,000. Head investigator on the case, Jim Rowley, was hospitalized shortly after White's conviction for high blood pressure that they attributed to the pressure of the Drake Diner case. However, the DMPD Department Achievement Committee named Jim Rowley "Top Cop of the Year for 1993" for his outstanding investigative work and determined effort to solve Des Moines' toughest and most publicized case.

In March, 1999, Cara McGrane's father, Tom, filed a lawsuit in the State of Washington asking the court to hold Roger and Elizabeth Cline liable under the theories of vicarious liability or a breach of duty to the general public for failing to properly secure their firearms – specifically the Grizzly that ended up with Joe White. In their defense, Clines stated that they went away for the weekend and left one of their firearms in the master bedroom, instead of locking it in the safe in their house. Their children had always been instructed not to enter the bedroom when the parents were away. The gun was left on a location known only to the parents and the children had also been instructed never to touch guns. The Clines had a standing rule that the children were never to have guests at their house in their absence. Nevertheless, Johanna invited a girlfriend and two young men to the house. When the Clines returned, they found the firearm, ammunition and jewelry missing and it was reported to the police.

McGrane's theory is that Johanna allowed Joseph White into the bedroom or she may have given the gun to him, which she denied in court. White's possession of the firearm resulted in the death of their daughter. On the Cline's motion, the trial court finally dismissed the suit. The court found that there are too many issues of legitimate public debate concerning the private ownership and storage of firearms for the court to impose potential liability upon firearm owners based solely on factors of ownership, theft, and subsequent criminal use of a firearm. The court also found that Johanna Cline was not acting *on behalf* of her parents by stealing or allowing the theft of the firearm and jewelry – there was no vicarious liability.

The Iowa Department of Corrections worked in conjunction with the Texas Bureau of Corrections addressing the problem of gang violence in their facilities by agreeing to a prisoner exchange. The exchange placed the most troublesome prisoners from each institution, including Joe White, in a "foreign" environment with the expectation that it would decrease the episodes of prison disruption and violence for each facility. The Iowa DOC contracted with an agency to transport six violent prisoners from Iowa to Texas in 1997. Reportedly, the transporters were older people with limited correctional experience who were coerced into stopping at a Texas rest area where the prisoners escaped. A convention of Texas State Troopers was being held nearby. The troopers were immediately summoned to aid in the search for the escaped inmates. All six were captured in a short time. They were returned to the Iowa system and the exchange program was discontinued immediately. As disruptive as he has been behind bars, there have been reports that Joseph White has been the victim of physical abuse in prison. His escape from custody in Texas made his case subject to federal jurisdiction.

White is now incarcerated for life in the ADX Florence Supermax.

The Florence Supermax, located in Florence, CO, is a 490 bed maximum-security federal prison. It houses the most dangerous prisoners in the Federal Bureau of Prisons system. Most of the inmates are kept 23 hours a day in solitary confinement in single occupant cells.

Notable inmates serving their sentences in the facility include Theodore "Ted" Kaczynski (The Unibomber), Terry Nichols (Oklahoma Building bomber), Zacarias Moussaoui (9/11 attack conspirator), Barry Mills (Aryan Brotherhood leader) and Eric Rudolph (Olympic Park bomber).

The murder weapon, the L.A.R.Grizzly, was never recovered.

About The Author

Pete Hale, a life-long resident of Des Moines, Iowa called upon his own experiences in law enforcement in writing The Drake Diner Murders.

He served on the Des Moines Police Department as a Senior Police Officer in the 1970's. He served in the U.S. Army with the 101st Airborne Division, fighting in Vietnam in 1967 - 1968. He was awarded the Bronze Star and the Air Medal. He then served with the 82nd Airborne Division, Fort Bragg, NC after his tour in Vietnam.

Pete lives in Des Moines, on the Southside, with his wife Lucia. He has two grown children and four grandchildren.

Notes

[1] Des Moines Register, "Police find killings difficult to solve", December 2, 1992, Page 1N.

[2] Des Moines Register, "Our love, memories of Cara", December 4, 1992, Page 6N.

[3] Des Moines Register, "Drake neighbors find reason for fear", December 1, 1992, Page 4M.

[4] Des Moines Register, Editorial, December 3, 1992, Page 16N.

[5] Behind the Badge, "Murder Will Out", 1999, Page 170.

[6] Des Moines Register, "Experts say they don't think the killer from Des Moines", December 2, 1992, Page 2M.

[7] Des Moines Register, "Our love, memories of Cara", December 4, 1992, Page 1N.

[8] Des Moines Register, "Defiant Drake area residents rally in support of the community", December 5, 1992, Page 1N.

[9] Des Moines Register, "Teen held in diner slaying", December 6, 1992, Page 1N.

[10] Des Moines Register, "Teens maintain their innocence in diner slaying", December 7, 1992, Page 1N.

[11] Des Moines Register, "Teens maintain their innocence in diner slaying", December 7, 1992, Page 1N.

[12] Des Moines Register, "Youth charged in two slayings at Drake Diner", December 8, 1992, Page 2N.

[13] Des Moines Register, "Rice: Big handguns should be banned", December 9, 1992, Page 1M.

[14] Des Moines Register, "Suspects relatives say they feel grief", December 10, 1992, Page 1N.

[15] Des Moines Register, "Slaying suspects spend loot at party", December 17, 1992, Page 1N.

[16] Des Moines Register. Gun permit requests rise after 2 slayings", December 19, 1992, Page 1N.

[17] Des Moines Register. Gun permit requests rise after 2 slayings", December 19, 1992, Page 1N.

[18] Des Moines Register, "Teen accused in diner slaying faces new charges in assault case", December 23, 1992, Page 1M.